BION

in

NEWYO...

and

SÃOPAULO

BION

in

NEW YORK

and

SÃO PAULO

THE ROLAND HARRIS TRUST LIBRARY
No. 10

CLUNIE PRESS
PERTHSHIRE

The Roland Harris Education Trust 1980

I.S.B.N. 902 965 13 1
First Published in 1980
Produced by Radavian Press, Reading

PREFACE

Wilfred Bion died in Oxford on November 8 1979 less than a week after he was diagnosed as suffering from myeloid leukaemia. The content of this book was approved by him in 1978.

The two series of discussions form an illuminating contrast: The 1979 South American visit was Bion's third to Sao Paulo and fourth to Brazil; his method of presenting his subject was, therefore, familiar to those taking part. The visit to New York in 1977 was his first.

It must be admitted that for those looking for cut-and-dried 'answers' Bion's method was inexplicable, frustrating and aggravating. Here was a man, thoroughly conversant with his subject, exceptionally articulate and therefore well able to supply questioners with what they wanted to hear—and he knew it. But he was steadfast in his respect for the truth and would not be persuaded against his better judgment to follow a course in which he could not respect himself.

He believed that "La réponse est le malheur de la question"; both in his professional and private life problems stimulated in him thought and discussion—never answers. His replies—more correctly, counter-contributions—were, in spite of their apparent irrelevance, an extension of the questions. His point of view is best illustrated in his own words:

"I don't know the answers to these questions—I wouldn't tell you if I did. I think it is important to find out for yourselves"

"I try to give you a chance to fill the gap left by me"

"I don't think that my explanation matters. What I would draw attention to is the *nature* of the problem."

"When I feel a pressure—I'd better get prepared in case you ask me some questions—I say, 'To hell with it, I'm not going to look up this stuff in Freud or anywhere else, or even in my past statement—I'll put up with it'. But of course I am asking you to put up with it too."

FRANCESCA BION
Editor

AUTHOR'S NOTE

I thank all who participated in these discussions with their objections and agreements. Many who read this book will feel that my replies are inadequate and incomplete. That they are inadequate I must admit; that they are incomplete I regard as a virtue especially if it stimulates the reader to complete the answers. I wish the reader as much enjoyment as I had in speaking; if it sends him to sleep may I wish him "Sweet Dreams and a profitable awakening".

W.R.B.

NEW YORK
1977

These talks, given in April 1977 under the auspices of the Institute for Psychoanalytic Training and Research (I.P.T.A.R.), took place on five consecutive evenings. There were two groups of participants; one attended talks One, Three and Five; the other, Two and Four. Although some roughnesses and repetitions, inevitable in impromptu expression, have been deleted it is hoped that the printed record is not misleading. A few passages have been added subsequently; these are marked [ ].

ONE

BION Well, here we are.

But where is 'here'? I remember a time when I was at an address —
some seventy years ago — which I called "Newbury House, Hadam
Road, Bishops Stortford, Hertfordshire, England, Europe.
Another small boy said to me, "You have left out 'The World' ". So I
put that in too. Since then I have been told by the astronomers that
we are part and parcel of a nebular universe, a spiral nebula to which
our solar system belongs. Astronomers can get away with a remark
like this; nobody complains that they are always 'inventing' new dis-
coveries. But, as Freud pointed out, this is not the case with doctors
or psycho-analysts. People say, "These doctors are always inventing
new diseases; then they treat them. It becomes a vested interest". But
nobody says "You astronomers invent a new universe and want
another telescope". I suppose it is because we feel it doesn't matter
very much what the Universe is.

I want now to narrow down the view, cutting out the various elements we regard as irrelevant. As analysts we look at what we call the
character or personality. This peculiar view — I won't say Freud
started it, but he gave it a considerable push — turns out to be a vast
universe of its own kind. We forget that the dimension which Freud
introduced into this scrutiny has caused a lot of trouble. We fail to
notice it because we are in the storm centre, unaware of the 'centre'
of which we are a part. But it is that disturbance with which we are
concerned.

What does it look like to us? When we go to our offices tomorrow
what do we expect to see? What are we going to look at? What is our
interpretation, our diagnosis? What is our interpretation of the facts
which our senses make available?

We assume that there is a mind, a personality. What does it look
like? What does it smell like? Does it present itself to our touch, our
feelings? Do we get any tactile impression? We know that so far we do
not; so far we cannot say, "I walk into this room blindfold and I can
feel a psychosis hitting up against my mind". What then is making
contact? Is there any way of verbalizing this? Is there any way of communicating this thing to each other? Hypothetically, yes. Hypothetically we can write papers, we can write books about it. But what *do*
we contact tomorrow? Can we say from what we contact, "I have

been here before; I have had this sensation before now'"? If so, what sensation?

Expanding our view again, taking the entire universe — I have been here before. Where? According to the astronomers this spiral nebula, of which our solar system is a part, is itself rotating; it is a long way from one side to the other and a long time, from our point of view, before we are at the same spot again — something like twice ten to the power of eight million light years — so far indeed that if we look towards the galactic centre there is nothing to see excepting the remnants of the Crab Nebula which is still in process of exploding. To us it looks immense because we are such ephemeral creatures.

Not forgetting that, but using it as a background, narrow down the view again and look at it through this microscopic, psycho-analytic view. We need to have some idea what we 'see', what we make contact with. It would be useful if we could feel there was something familiar about it and say, "I have seen this before", or "I have had this experience before".

To return to my own private life: When I was small I used to be regarded by grown-ups as a very odd child who was always asking questions. I was made to recite a poem:

> 'I keep six honest serving-men
> They taught me all I knew;
> Their names are What and Why and When
> And How and Where and Who.
> I send them over land and sea,
> I send them east and west;
> But after they have worked for me,
> I give them all a rest.'*

It was considered to be extraordinarily amusing that I had to recite this piece of verse. I could not see the joke myself. I was told I was just like the Elephant's Child who asked these questions — and like a fool I asked another one. I said, "Who was the Elephant's Child's father?" That was not popular; it was not amusing. But I was not making a joke. I decided I had better be careful not to ask too many questions; it took me a long time to dare to start asking questions again. The person who made it easier for me was John Rickman who was the first psycho-analyst I ever met. I am still at it—I don't think it is any more popular now than it ever was.

To return to this simple poem of Kipling's—"I give them all a rest". When we are in the office with a patient we have to dare to rest. It is difficult to see what is at all frightening about that, but it is. It is

---

*Rudyard Kipling, *The Elephant's Child*, Just So Verses.

difficult to remain quiet and let the patient have a chance to say whatever he or she has to say. It is frightening for the patient — and the patient hates it. We are under constant pressure to say something, to admit that we are doctors or psycho-analysts or social workers; to supply some box into which we can be put complete with a label. So the patient tries to diagnose the analyst, and the analyst hopes that somehow he will have a chance to "see a pattern emerge". I use that phrase deliberately; Freud was most impressed by Charcot's use of it.*

We have to focus our attention on the individual. It is no good talking about the astronomical universe; it is no good talking about the cosmos. But to suggest that we are people with a prejudice in favour of having respect for the individual is a dangerous thing to do because it will not be tolerated easily by the group, the crowd, the nation or the race. It is as well to be clear about this: We are involved in a philosophical prejudice in favour of a person, in favour of the uniqueness of the human individual. There will be an emotional pressure against each single one of us who dares to attach importance to an individual and who dares to be an individual himself. We may long to say, "I'm American", or British or Freudian or Jungian or Kleinian — any label which is 'respectable'. But every psycho-analyst has to have the temerity, and the fortitude which goes with it, to insist on the right to be himself and to have his own opinion about this strange experience which he has when he is aware that there is another person in the room. Pressure against this is considerable; your senses tell you that it is your office; you are used to the windows here, the furniture there; there is every pressure to make you feel you are at home. It is difficult to resist that. I have suggested this: Discard your memory; discard the future tense of your desire; forget them both, both what you knew and what you want, to leave space for a new idea. A thought, an idea unclaimed, may be floating around the room searching for a home. Amongst these may be one of your own which seems to turn up from your insides, or one from outside yourself, namely, from the patient.

Here is a dismal story: the patient has been coming to you for the last five, ten years. If you were honest you would have to say that you are sick to death of the sight of that patient; and if the patient is honest he would have to say he is sick to death of hearing about psycho-analysis or seeing his analyst. It is not polite to talk in that way; nor is it helpful. We should retain civilized and conventional politeness. It exceeds the limits of the necessary minimum conditions for psycho-analysis to resort to violence such as breaking furniture, though an analyst may tolerate such behaviour temporarily. A child

*Freud, S. *Introductory Lectures on Psycho-analysis*

— of whatever age — can be expected to behave reasonably politely. [Each analyst must be clear in his own mind what for him are the minimum conditions necessary (MCN) in which he and his patient can do the work.]

Let us widen our view, taking a biological vertex. So far the human animal has been extremely destructive; it hunts in groups, in herds, and has managed to kill opposition from other dangerous animals — even tigers and lions. [Analyst and analysand are alone in the same room. The MCN are that both behave in a conventionally civilized and polite manner. They are still dangerous animals, so we can see that the limitation proposed by psycho-analysis itself restricts their behaviour. We also indicate (and provoke, albeit unintentionally) primitive behaviour.

The psycho-analytic conversation is itself an experience of conflict between the phenomena to which attention is drawn and the MCN for the work. If this fact, often unobserved, were allowed for it would make it possible to understand why the analyst and the analysand are fatigued by the strain of a psycho-analysis.] Annoyance between analyst and analysand is likely. We can use technical terms like 'transference' and 'counter-transference', provided they illuminate rather than obscure. But the thing itself doesn't go away because we have given it a name; whatever they are called, the feelings of the couple remain.

Starting from the moment of birth we are always supposed to be learning to behave in a civilized way. At an early age we have already learnt not only *not* to be ourselves but also *who* to be; we have a well established label, diagnosis, interpretation of who we are. But the *facts* continue to exist. What the patient says can be used by the analyst as a free association. [This may be mistaken by the analysand as a way of ignoring the facts which he has communicated. It is necessary for the analyst to be clear in his mind that this is not so.] In due course a pattern will emerge which can then in its turn be interpreted. As a by-product the patient can discover who he is. So few people think that it is important to be introduced to themselves, but the one partner the patient can never get rid of while that patient is alive is himself.

Q.* How do you proceed in helping the patient to discover his true self?

B. It is difficult to borrow from a newly developed 'sense' — of self awareness — to illuminate the fundamental and basic thing. I try to give myself a chance to absorb that basic thing. Our common senses tell us that there is another person in the room; the basic 'thing' — not

*Question

the 'common sense' — is what I wish to make explicit. I cannot describe what a 'person' is, but I am sure there is such a thing, and I am sure it is not adequate to describe what presents itself to my eyes, my ears or even what could be recorded by a video-tape. It is too crude; there is something else in the room.

If you show a musician a sheet of music he can see the black marks on a white background but he behaves as if there is something beyond that.

The painter sees a field of poppies — which everybody has seen — and paints a picture of them. You may see a reproduction of it — it doesn't mean a thing. If you walk into the Jeux de Paumes in Paris and see the painting itself, you think "I never saw a field of poppies until now; *now* I know what it looks like" — it is an emotional experience, not a report on one. How does a great painter manage to use pigments and canvas to give countless people an idea of what a field of poppies looks like?

Shakespeare writes a simple piece of prose: "The raven himself is hoarse that croaks the fatal entrance of Duncan under my battlements". All the words are simple; "battlements" is the longest one and doesn't take a moment to look up in the dictionary. But "The raven is hoarse that croaks the fatal entrance of Duncan under my battlements" — that is something else. What else is it?

I am well aware that you are not going to see a Shakespeare or a Monet in your office; the person will be disguised as Mr. or Mrs. X of such-and-such address. Don't be taken in by that; don't be taken in by the fact that you think you have seen this patient before—you have not. What you have seen before doesn't matter. What does matter is what we, the analyst and the patient, have *not* seen before. Prince Andrei, in *War and Peace*, says on hearing a remark, "That is sooth, accept it — that is sooth, accept it." We likewise can feel, "Yes, that is true. That interpretation is right; that observation is correct." That is contact with the *thing itself*. Unfortunately it doesn't happen as often as we would like; the two personalities do not often meet. But they may meet closely enough to be aware that there is something more in the room than a computer can process.

The infant knows what it is to have raging emotions — things to which we give crude names, like fear, depression, love, hate — but it doesn't know what to call them; by the time it has mastered articulate speech it has forgotten what it feels like to be an infant. So we, who have reached this stage of being capable of articulate speech, have almost forgotten what it feels like to be human. We spend too many impressionable years in learning how to be just like everybody else — not how to be ourselves. Now we spend too many years in the intellectual stratosphere. But despite what we have learned, certain 'crude' feelings are still able to make themselves felt; if they can dare, the analytic couple can still feel love and hate.

The analyst is trying to help the patient to dare to be himself, to dare to have enough respect for his personality to be that person. The analytic experience, in spite of all the appearance of comfort — comfortable couch, comfortable chairs, warmth, good lighting – is in fact a stormy, emotional experience for the two people. If you are an officer in a battle you are supposed to be sane enough to be scared; but you are supposed also to be capable of thinking. It sounds ridiculous to say that people sitting in a comfortable room in full peace time have to be capable of anything — but they do. The analyst is supposed to remain articulate and capable of translating what he is aware of into a comprehensible communication. That means that he has to have a vocabulary which the patient may be able to understand if given a chance to hear what the analyst has to say. It sounds absurdly simple — so simple that it is hard to believe how difficult it is.

The language we use is so debased that it is like a coin which has been so rubbed that it is impossible to distinguish its value. "I'm terribly frightened" says the patient. What about it? Terribly. Frightened. These words are commonplace. But I now become alert when I hear that word "terribly" because it is so worn. It's terrible weather; it's terrible this; it's terrible that; the word means nothing. [When the patient becomes aware of the analyst's attention he will find a more arcane way to say "terribly frightened" — perhaps even a 'psycho-analytic way'. The game of hide-and-seek will enter a new phase.]

O.* When psycho-analysis works I think it gives the patient a sense of conviction of what it is about. I feel our efforts should be directed towards finding what is lost, what is *not* stated.

B. What you say seems to come near to what Melanie Klein tried to say; it illuminated things so much that it revealed still greater vistas of darkness, unilluminated areas. In psycho-analysis we are always unveiling still further domains of ignorance, darkness, the Void.

Melanie Klein said that patients have omnipotent phantasies, that they split off parts of the personality and project them into the breast. She meant what she said and I think that was correct — as far as it went. What I am not so sure about it that it is *only* an omnipotent phantasy. I have experienced the situation in which the patient can arouse in me feelings which have a simple explanation. You could say, "Anybody would know why the patient makes you feel like that; you need to have more analysis". That is true, but it is not the whole truth. I think that the patient does something to the

*Observation

analyst and the analyst does something to the patient; it is not just an omnipotent phantasy.

When a pattern emerges which the analyst wants to communicate to the analysand he has to use a formula that the analysand is capable of receiving. An expert diamond cutter can cut the facets in such a way that light which is reflected onto the diamond is thrown back again — with increased brilliance — by the same route. That is why the fine precious stone sparkles. [This model is itself an example of my attempt to make clear to you what I wish to illuminate. The analysand, by coming, gives the analyst an opportunity to observe his behaviour — including both what he says and does not say. Out of the totality of what the analyst is aware of he detects a pattern. When it is sufficiently clear to him he can decide whether he can convey it in a language comprehensible to the analysand, augmented in a manner analogous to the model.] Thus the analyst can hope to reflect back the same illumination given him by the analysand, but with greater intensity.

Patients sometimes wonder why we are so uncommunicative; why, for example, we don't tell them whether we are married, or whether we have any children. We don't tell them these things for good reasons; they can get so filled with knowledge about the analyst that there is no room for the exercise of their own conjectures and, therefore, for the development of their own capacity to think. [An inherent difficulty in analysis is that any interpretation tells the patient something about the analyst. It would be no easier if the analyst deliberately concealed his true personality. All that he can do is to avoid or allow for that distortion.]

I can say to the patient, "You are feeling that I am — such-and-such"; that is not information about myself as the analyst. I hope that the patient will be able to recognise it as his own idea — hitherto unrecognized. It requires courage on the part of the patient because he is terrified of learning something about himself which he has never wanted to know and which he has spent his life not being aware of—probably from before birth—trying to learn what he *ought* to be. Where does this 'ought' come from? Have we, as analysts, told them what they 'ought' to be? If, as we hope, we have not then this 'ought' must have come from somewhere else. *Immediately* it has come from the patient; where has it come from *mediately*? One hopes to be able to give the patient a chance of finding out.

Q. Is there any way of knowing if you are not kidding yourself?

B. [This question touches the profound problem of Truth. Through the ages anyone who has felt the urge to know the truth has rapidly found himself confronted by this question — can any human being validate what he thinks is true? Psycho-analysis cannot be practised without becoming aware of that problem; at every juncture of the analytic experience it could be expanded thus:-

1. What is the analysand's behaviour?
2. What aspect of it enshrines the truth?
3. Have we observed his behaviour correctly?
4. In so far as we have observed it correctly what have we observed?
5. Knowing what we know now, is any human being who aspires to the truth engaged on more than a fool's errand?
   I doubt that any of us can escape this; even apodeictic 'knowledge' is vulnerable.]

To return to the problem of language: [Terms such as 'counter-transference' have suffered debasement through the popularization of psycho-analysis. It is probably no worse than the popularization of physical medicine and surgery which leads to applications of a home-made poltice to a cancerous sore.] One of the essential points about counter-transference is that it is *unconscious*. People talk about 'making use of' their counter-transference; they cannot make any use of it because they don't know what it is. There *is* such a thing as my emotional reaction to the patient; I can hope that through my awareness of the fact that I have human characteristics like prejudice and bigotry I may be more tolerant and allow the patient to feel if my interpretation is or is not correct. That is a transient experience. It is one reason for calling it 'transference'; it is a feeling or thought or idea you have on your way to somewhere else. When you are in the presence of something which you have learnt to call a transference can you feel more precisely what it is at the time? It depends on what the patient says to you being allowed to enter into you, allowed to bounce off, as it were, your inner being and get reflected out.

Q. Are you suggesting that it is not so much your reaction to the patient in terms of your interpretation — which is undoubtedly contaminated by your counter-transference — but rather the atmosphere in which the patient is provided with the opportunity to transfer and to explore being?

B. I think the patient ultimately has the chance of learning that. He may get the idea that there is something to be said for analysis and for the time and money spent on it. The time it takes cannot be measured by the months or years the patient was coming to your office; the after effects of that experience persist.

Q. Doesn't the language of psycho-analysis take one away from psychic reality? Since it is mostly sensuous imagery, and psychic reality is essentially non-sensuous, one has to be careful how one uses psycho-analytic thoughts for language.

B. The founder of University College, London, was a man who had studied philosophy at Oxford. His summary of that experience was that the only thing he had ever learnt was dissimulation and lying. Indeed, one of the earliest achievements of articulate speech is just that; how to make a fool of other people — which often involves making a fool of oneself as well. So your question is a fundamental one — how is verbal communication, which has such a long history of use for purposes of deception, dissimulation and lying, to be reconstituted to further the progress to truth. It is a question which you have to answer for yourself; you have to find out what the vocabulary is that comes most naturally to you and which you can continue to use, and so restore some of its value for this particular purpose of helping people rather than sinking them.

Q. Do you work with families?

B. I prefer them not to get through my office door. I cannot of course guarantee to keep them out mentally. I consider I am trying to analyse the patient; what his family are doing to him I don't know and I can do nothing about them. I feel there is a lot of unexplored and unexhausted territory which can be investigated only analytically. If you think you can cope with the further experience that an entire family could bring I do not see why you should not do so; it is not my choice. I attach a great deal of importance to the experience that I am permitted to have if the patient will come to my office and stay there for fifty minutes. The moment the patient is out of my sight and hearing the value of the experience falls off fast. Hearsay evidence is worth very little to me. I hear all sorts of things about myself, about my patients, which are to me not much more than a meaningless noise. "It is a tale told by an idiot, full of sound and fury, signifying nothing." The chance you are given by exposure to the patient's personality is invaluable; it is difficult to know how to get fifty minutes worth out of it.

Q. Your work with groups suggests that within that matrix there are certain basic assumptions going on. Could you not conceive of a family situation as a group situation? Might there be some basic assumptions at work with all sorts of underlying archaic processes that are worth exploring too?

B. Yes, there are. Freud said it is important to analyse the Oedipal situation. What is the Oedipal situation? Who are the characters? Father, mother, child? Can you be sufficiently exposed to the change that occurs when a patient walks into your office to be able to communicate first of all with yourself? To do this you have to forget, denude your mind of what you know, so as to have yourself free to what is going on. Then as you watch the 'screen', can you see any pattern flicker into position? Who are the characters who are in search of an author? You will have to be the author; and when you have this play clear you could mention it to the patient—that would then be your interpretation. I have also described it as "thoughts in search of a thinker"; I have to be exposed to it on the off-chance that some stray thought might lodge itself in my mind— or if not mine, the patient's. It might then be verbalized.

If you find mathematics provides you with a more convenient language — I am still talking about your communication with yourself — then you might decide a triangle would represent it. But so many people have heard of 'the eternal triangle'; it has become a debased, meaningless phrase.

Again falling back on a model: The ancient Egyptians discovered that if you knot a piece of cord in the proportions of 2, 4 and 5 and join them up in a triangle, then you have a right angle and can build places like Thebes. Pythagoras — or so they say — discovered the Pythagorean theory. It is illuminating, a mental can-opener; it gives you a chance of opening your mind and, if you are lucky, finding inside a thought or two which might come in useful for an interpretation. Can you then verbalize it in such a way that the patient would understand your language? I am familiar with thinking I have discovered an interpretation, and have taken a long time giving it, only to be told by the patient, "I don't know what you are talking about." People are educated to believe that they ought to behave in a civil manner, that personal remarks are impolite. It is difficult to realize that the patient often cannot stand hearing what we have to say; the analytic conversation with which we are familiar is not familiar to him. Although the words are in common use the meaning that they are to convey is not; the patient is being exposed to an experience which is usually nasty and which is also unknown.

Q. How does it differ from other situations in which one person is communicating with another, like that of a mother with her child or other didactic relationships?

B. What makes it unique is that there are two unique people in the room. The more respect one has for the individual the more obvious it is that there is no other 'you' and no other 'him' or 'her'. On the other hand, there is something wrong with an analysis which doesn't remind both the analyst and analysand of real life. What is it about if it has no resemblance to the universe we live in — a universe of ideas and thoughts and feelings? If we can get near to verbalizing and describing what we want to convey, then the patient can recognize that we are talking about what is available here and now reminding him that similar situations exist elsewhere which are likely to occur over and over again. We are not talking about something which happens only in an office or only within the limits of what we call psycho-analysis, any more than one could say that a^2+b^2+2ab is only an algebraic formula. It is of application; these proportions exist in different situations; situations where people want to build vast temples which stand up by themselves at right angles to the earth and to the foundations.

O. I wondered why you said it was a "nasty" experience. You also said that the patient and the analyst can get bored; at another point you said that it was a very exciting experience. It is clear, listening to you, that you consider it a special and intimate experience.

B. I can take one of the examples you mention. I remember a patient who was so boring that I became fascinated by how he did it. How could this man converse with me in a way that was nearer to what I would call 'pure boredom' than anything I had ever experienced? That is why it is fascinating; your curiosity is stirred up.

Q. Did you figure it out?

B. I would like to be able to write a book on the hundred and one versions of boredom — if I had the skill or the time to do it. If you can stand the boredom of it you may be able, like the patient, to put up with it long enough for something to flicker into place, something which you could then translate into words. The patient keeps on talking about something which one could describe as a transference relationship, but the two things which might anchor it are missing; there is only the bit in between. It becomes a sort of 'pure' psychoanalysis; it is nothing but transference with nobody else in the room — and that is extraordinarily boring to hear. You recognize after a time that you are being told something by the patient, but never a fact within sight or hearing. You know nothing about the patient; you know nothing about the patient's private life. What interpretation are you to give? In a sense you could say it is an analogy, but a pure analogy; not the two things on either side, only the link in between. Translated into biological terms: What is this? A breast? A penis? No baby? No mother? Only the thing in between? Is this 'pure' psycho-analysis; all sex, but not a relationship between two people? This peculiar situation is not simply a question of semantics, not a question of learning grammar. This is an actual event which is taking place in front of you, a demonstration of what joins two people, but with neither person present—they are both missing. What then is the link? If we don't bother about the two people, what about this thing in between? If it is neither a breast nor a penis, could it possibly be a vagina? Could it be a non-object. It is possible for what we biologically call a 'woman' to have a sexual relationship with another person?

TWO

B. "Well"....... "I mean to say"........ "You know"......... I can go on like that for hours. It is the wreckage, the remnants of thought. Patients often want to tell you something, but all they have with which to do it are the remnants of articulate speech. So the first thing you are confronted with is the remains of a culture or civilization. We try to be as conscious, as wide awake, as logical as we know; to have all our wits, all our experience about us to do the work of psycho-analysis. But is that state of mind one which can make contact with a different state of mind?

Freud gave meaning to words like 'conscious' and 'unconscious', drawing attention to the fact that there is a state of mind which is different from what we usually call 'conscious'. I am not sure that he made a clear cut distinction between what he was talking about adjectivally — unconscious modes of procedure, unconscious modes of thought—and *the* unconscious as if there were such a thing. These concepts, these theories match up with what most people vaguely recognize, partly because we all think we know the language, but we know a debased language— a vague language.

I don't think this idea of *the* unconscious, or even the idea of unconscious thoughts or ideas, extends far enough. It is surprising how far Freud got with those theories and the extent to which he made his own work redundant. He opened up still further areas of experience which cannot be treated in the way in which we attempt to treat neuroses and those phenomena in which this idea of the unconscious and unconscious thoughts — the substantive and adjectival words—are indicated.

I draw attention to the existence of what seem to be primordial ideas and feelings which have *never been conscious*. They are different from ideas which have been conscious at some time and have been repressed, or have been transformed into something which is unconscious. That realm which we often think of as being somewhat irrational is in fact rational — if seen from another vertex. If you have an experience about which you can do nothing you forget it — it is obvious common sense. If you have a tooth-ache and there is nobody to look after your teeth — forget it. If you have an ache in your mind, forget it. But psycho-analysis seems to indicate that that is not good enough because when this thing has been forgotten — as I think, correctly — it goes on leading an independent existence and then gives rise to symptoms and signs of its activity although we are not conscious of it, although we have 'forgotten' it. Does the same thing apply to something which has never at any time been conscious?

As I said before * patients sometimes behave as if they were in fact — not phantasy — splitting off parts of their personality and pushing them into my insides. Sometimes I wonder why I begin to feel angry or alarmed in a session; I am not able to dismiss the feeling that the patient is doing something to me, actually having an effect upon me. We can deal with this sort of patient by saying "Psychotic — incurable. It's time the analysis was terminated because this is beyond analytic capacity". We hope some psychiatric hospital will kindly take charge of the patient and lock him up safely. In that way these awkward patients cease to disturb our peace; we have them safely under lock and key; we have them mentally categorized in a mental box; they are psychotics, they are finished and done with — but the sufferer remains. To succumb to that impulse gradually erodes the psycho-analyst's integrity.

Suppose an intelligent, powerfully mentally equipped man and woman have biological sexual intercourse and bring together ova and spermatozoa which initiate cell division. According to the embryologists, cell divisions take place and at the 3 Somite stage optic and auditory pits are formed. In this period the cell division is going on in a watery fluid which is polluted. (I am taking as pure fluid extra-cellular fluid which seems to have the composition which sea water had before it became sea water. The extra-cellular fluid is the nearest thing you could possibly imagine to an absolute stage when the world was surrounded with water before the water was polluted with earth products.) Changes in pressure in this watery medium are easily communciated. The amniotic fluid can be subjected to changes of pressure through uterine contractions for example; there may also be pressures extraneous to the mother — she can be

*see p. 14

shouted at, pushed about. If you put pressure on your eyeball—and if someone is so unkind as to do it suddenly and violently— you can be said to 'see stars'; you get an impression of light. But that is an anomalous response. [One day the remnants of that anomalous response can emerge with a force that disconcerts both patient and analyst; The analyst is told that the patient suffers from intense, bright colours or fortification patterns or, possibly, migrainous headaches.]

When do the auditory or optic pits become functional? When is there some kind of primordial sight or hearing? by the time there is an autonomic or sympathetic nervous system — a 'thalamic' brain — the embryo may be experiencing something which one day might be called 'hate' or 'fear'; [contemporaneously an impulse to fight or run away. The thalamus and limbic nuclei will one day be the origins of fear and aggression, dancing and combat. For convenience we can describe this briefly as 'sub-thalamic' behaviour.]

Suppose the fetus arrives at what the obstetricians call 'full term'. Does the fetus have to be born before it has a personality or a mind? Conversely, does man have a mind? I see no reason to doubt that the full term fetus has a personality. It seems to me to be gratuitously non-sensical to suppose that the physical fact of birth is something which creates a personality which was not in existence before then. It is much more reasonable to suppose that this fetus, or even embryo, has a mind which one day could be described as highly intelligent. [We shall have to consider this point further if we have an emotional impulse to relegate one of our patients to a category of 'hopeless' or 'psychotic'. Before acting on such an impulse we need to ask ourselves whether 'hopeless' or 'psychotic' is a description which illuminates *our* state of mind rather than that of the patient.]

Q. What about the question of myelination of nerve endings, the idea that there can be some sort of neurological recording in an integrated centre in terms of registering information within the young person's mind?

B. [Is it possible that the hypochondrial areas attempt to communicate with the cerebrum, that the autonomic nervous system tries to communicate with the voluntary system, that the body tries to communicate with the mind— assuming that there is a mind?] Physicians and surgeons interpret these pains: It is difficult to do. For example, a patient once said to me, "I've got water on the knee doctor". I palpated it and sure enough there seemed to be a bursitis. The patient was a charwoman who used to do a good deal of kneeling and it mattered to her that her knee was giving her trouble. She also complained about some difficulty in holding her water. She said,

"When I cough I always pees a little". She gave a little cough and said, "There, I peed again then". I said, "As a matter of fact you have coughed quite a lot here haven't you?" "Oh, that's nothing. I've always had this cough". At this point I had a vague idea that I had come across the lymphatic system in Grey's Anatomy; I said, "We'd like to have an X-ray of your chest". There it was. Foggy patches; obscurity. The path. lab. report on the knee fluid was 'tubercular'; the tubercle had tracked down from the lungs and turned up in the knee.

[That diagnosis was based on sophisticated medical theory. My 'vague idea' was a rational conjecture. Could there have been some direct mental link in the patient's mind between a sore knee and a cough reflex?] Is there mental 'stuff' distinct from the physical network of communication? The theories of Freud, Klein, Abraham and others presuppose that there is. I subscribe to that belief and the experience of psycho-analysis is to me convincing. It is, however, equally clear to me that this is a 'probability' and not a 'certainty'. An austere judgment would not concede 'certainty' to the lymphatic system; that is typical of the still unexplored means of communication, the myelinated fibres you have just mentioned, the neurological mechanism, the para-sympathetic system, the system by which the body makes what it has to say noticeable up at the cranial end for which superiority is claimed, even a social superiority, to what goes on at our tail ends.

I suggest that there is something which can communicate itself from the full term fetus, and possibly earlier than that, to the mind as we know it. Why should the symptom, the sign of some trouble or defect, not track its way through channels — about which we as yet know nothing — to appear in the area of articulate speech? In other words, the articulate speech betrays a symptom which then we attempt to analyse. Would it be possible to say that certain mental articulate symptoms, if correctly interpreted, could lead a surgeon or physician directly to a physically disturbed organ. In the optic chiasma so many channels are close to each other — the basal nuclei and the basal ganglia can be interrupted as they would be by surgical interference in a lobotomy. Similarly a tumor there betrays itself in a variety of manners. It might be possible to say, "The way this patient talks to me shows symptoms of a physical disorder which are as clear to me as are the meanings of a sign like pallor, signs of anaemia". Following psycho-analytic principles, it is clear to me that the analyst should be alert to the tracking of symptoms in both directions. [The problem is not a mind with one track, but a track which is one-way.] If certain symptoms can make themselves emerge on what we call 'conscious, rational levels of thought', then conscious, rational levels of thought should be able to be made operative at the point of origin of the 'dis-ease'. Is it possible to make an interpretation which also tracks its way back by the same path to the origin of the trouble? If so, then psycho-analysis may be able to have some effect on things which at present appear to be inaccessible to treatment.

Q. If infants or patients do not simply have a phantasy that they are splitting off parts of their personality and evacuating them into mother or analyst but are actually doing it, what do you see happening? What is it that they do?

B. I take refuge in the idea of the Grid in this way:- Things which are called material can be regarded as being outside our province because they are facts of physical make-up. But — and here I am entering into grounds which I am sure would be controversial, and rightly so — I would also, besides these theoretically supposed imaginary beta- and alpha-elements, now suppose that thought enters into a phase which I could call *primordial*. I could say that the primordial thought also betrays itself here — I am talking about *us* — but now I would call it a speculative imagination. This kind of thought has nothing to do with 'evidence' — it is speculation. I encourage people to indulge their speculative imagination; there is a lot to be said for it before it turns into something a scientist might call 'evidence'. The sort of things which float about in this area of speculative imagination are rationalizations, phantasies, probabilities — not facts. This analytic activity upon which we are engaged does not seem at present to be supported by apodeictic evidence, but I think we are justified in saying that probably psycho-analysis is some use, probably the outcome of certain conversations which I have had together with somebody who is not me has been responsible for initiating further development. A diagnosis like 'psychotic' or 'borderline psychotic' does not allow room for elaboration, speculation, conjecture; it limits the possibilities of expansion. Analysis should not be so restricted that there is no room for development and growth. I can imagine — an imaginative conjecture — that the walls of the uterus might be so restricting that there is no alternative but for the mother to evacuate the creature which is inside, and for the creature which is inside to get out and make an adjustment from life in a watery fluid to life in a gaseous fluid. Then the parents likewise must develop, from husband and wife to father and mother, otherwise there will not be 'space' in which the neonate can develop.

Q. Coming back to the question of how you know about the possible projection from the patient into the analyst, whether it really happens, what about the way the analyst feels? The analyst, who usually feels comfortable, pleasant, suddenly in the middle of a session feels irrationally angry. Is that something the patient is doing to the analyst? Is that a counter-transference? Is that evoked?

B. What we *feel* is as near to fact as we are ever likely to get in this extraordinary occupation. While we are prepared to argue about the various ideas that we have, we are not prepared to argue about "what it feels like to be me". I can compare what it feels like to be me with what somebody else *says* that I am feeling like. The patient knows much more about what it feels like to be him or her than any analyst. So it is important to work on the basis that the best colleague you are ever likely to have — besides yourself — is not an analyst or supervisor or parent, but the patient; that is the one person on whom you can rely with confidence to be in possession of the vital knowledge. Why he doesn't simply make use of it I don't know. The human being is an animal which is dependent on a mate. In analysis it is a temporary mate; when it comes to life itself one would prefer to find somebody not oneself with whom to go through the rest of one's living days. The biological unit is a couple.

O. You talk about the mother 'evacuating' the fetus, the patient 'evacuating' either into the mother or the analyst. Then you say that the patient can tell us whether or not our interpretation is correct. It would seem as if the feeling or material the patient has evacuated still remains very much with the patient so that he can either tell us we are correct or incorrect, or whether it is rubbish. I am trying to understand what you mean by 'evacuation' in that sense.

B. I don't think you will ever understand that except in your office. There at least it is possible to have an opinion as to what it is. You can narrow down your view as if you changed your telescope for a microscope directing it in the area where you would be likely to find an answer to that question. I can easily indulge in speculative imagination and say I think the patient does evacuate something, but it is worse than useless if what I say is used as a substitute for the analyst's own observation.

Q. Reading your work, it is obvious that you choose your language extremely carefully. Re-phrasing the concept of evacuation and some other terms, what is lost from your idea if I say, "The patient who is not in touch with certain feelings, hasn't even got them articulated but experiences them at some level, is nevertheless very skilled in subtle ways at stimulating these feelings in another person"? Does that lose some of the meaning?

B. Looking at it in a highly intellectual way, one can make some use of Kant's idea: Intuition without concept is blind; concept without intuition is empty. Translating that into familiar language I could say that some patients are describing a fact intuitively when they say, "I am terrified", or "I am bothered by a stammer", and you hear no stammer at all — but the patient does. That intuition remains blind because he has not been able to match it with a concept. [Your version, your interpretation is the right one if it makes what you observe clear to your patient; to use *my* version would be incorrect.]

Q. You said we can make certain assumptions about the vestiges of the early impressions, both pre-natal and post-natal, but you spoke about a patient who was provoking anger in you. Could you give us a clinical example of how you would handle that — whether you relate it to the vestiges, whether you relate it to what you are feeling?

B. I doubt it, because what I would think of would be what I would like to believe I did.

Q. We could start with that—what would you like to believe you did? What would you tell the patient?

B. I would *try* to tell the patient what he had told me. The patient says, "I had a terrible dream last night in which I was having inter-course with my wife". I could say, "If that is what you were doing what are you telling me this for? What you did or what you dreamed is a matter of no importance. You must be trying to tell me something which *is* of importance because I don't think you are coming here to waste your time and money sitting in my office. I suggest that this story of yours has a meaning which is not yet known to either of us." *That* unknown is what requires illumination. The ordinary meaning doesn't cease to exist, but it is not important. This apparent statement of fact is actually a formulation of a question; it is a question disguised as a fact; it is covered up; it *sounds* like a fact. And when the patient says he "dreamed" it he is also claiming that it is a fact of the kind with which we are all familiar; it is socially acceptable; we are permitted to dream things like this; it is excused.

Q. In this hypothetical situation in which you tell the patient you don't know and he doesn't know, what would happen?

B. The answer to that is again, "I don't know".

Q. What would you tell him?

B. What I said I did; it was an expression of precisely what I mean. It may be a defective and inadequate and insufficient way of saying it, but I know of no other; and I think it is fair to assume that the patient knows no other way of saying it. If these thoughts are not in fact limited to the times when the person is asleep, if the patient has that same so-called 'dream' in broad daylight when he is wide awake, then somebody is liable to call it an hallucination or a delusion or a psychotic state. So there is a great deal to be said for saying "I dreamed it — it was only when I was off my guard".

After a time it becomes unmistakable that the way in which you talk to your patients seems to have an effect on them. Nobody can tell you that — you have to find it out for yourself. You have to be a practising analyst before you discover that it is worth your while talking to patients in the way that *you* talk to them — never mind whether it is sanctified by appearing in one of the Collected Works. That experience convinces you that it is worth while having some respect for your Self, for what you think and imagine and speculate. There is a curious kind of conviction about these occasions where what you say has an effect which is recognizably similar to your theories. A 'marriage' is taking place between you and you; a marriage between your thoughts and your feelings. The intuition which is blind and the concept when is empty can get together in a way which makes a complete mature thought.

Q. Earlier * you suggested that current theories of borderline states don't allow room to increase the patient's space. Could you explain that?

B. The status of what I am saying is speculative imagination; I have no supporting facts, but it seems to me to be worth labelling as 'probable': If the germ plasm is potentially perceptive, having derived from both these supposedly perceptive parents, then I can imagine that even in the womb that creature becomes aware of certain 'things' which are 'not self'. For example, I could suggest to you here, "Don't let's say a thing; let's shut the windows, make this place as silent as we can." What do we hear? If that could be carried out as an experiment then we could hear our heartbeat, the surge of blood in the arteries. It is possible that the fetus is aware of a primordial 'sight', of light, and can much dislike these impingements of experiences which seem to come from outer space — sensations of light, sensations of noise — and also from somewhere which may appear to be internal — the heartbeat, the blood rushing through the arteries. That might all be so intolerable that the fetus would — to use our conscious terminology — forget it, get rid of it, have nothing whatever to do with it. Then the infant is born; but this inheritance of great potential intelligence still survives. So the highly intelligent infant can learn the trick of behaving exactly and precisely in the way in which it is supposed to behave. To take a disastrous example: Leopold and

*see p. 24

Loeb decided to commit the perfect crime. In English law there used to be a touchstone called the MacNaughton Rules: Can the patient distinguish between right and wrong? Of course he can. You cannot expect highly intelligent people not to have learnt the trick of being able to know the difference between right and wrong. So there they are — on the first step towards conviction because they appear to be responsible people. I suspect that the experience of birth is too severe; what they did potentially, when they were embryos or fetuses, is no longer available to them. They do not have this fundamental feeling, knowledge of the difference between right and wrong. There has to be some ability to make a distinction between right and wrong, between real truth or compassion, and real evil — and that is different from knowing what people *call* the difference between right and wrong.

Q. You have written about the assumption of a psychotic core in each individual. Is this somehow related to pre-birth experience, to intra-uterine experience?

B. I think the intra-uterine experience is one which we have got used to forgetting. We like to feel that we are born and become intelligent and rational human beings, that the 'state of mind' when we are awake and conscious is superior to the 'state of mind' when we are asleep. We have a prejudice against the other state of mind — that is to say, the one in which we are not. So we try to keep the caesura in good repair; to change it into more psycho-analytic terms, to keep our resistance in good working order to act as an impermeable membrane through which thoughts and feelings and ideas of which we have disapproved at one time cannot penetrate. At the same time the thoughts and feelings that we did know at some time still strive to break loose. I could put it like this: We are all bad analysts, but every bad analyst has a good analyst inside him struggling to break free — and we hate it. We say, "My God, I'm having a breakdown! Thanks to this frightful analyst of mine my defences have been weakened and now I'm going to turn into some sort of monster and shall get locked up or commit a murder. If I'm going to commit a murder I'll start on my analyst before someone starts on me". This seems to be a situation in which there is an attempt to break through into freedom; *and* an attempt to prevent anything of the kind from happening. None of us can be free from hatred of analysis and the analytic experience, whether it is engendered by our own knowledge and experience, or whether by the sort of thing which is said to us by a patient who wears his id outside and his ego and superego tucked away inside; and who also behaves in a way which makes it clear that his is the proper state of mind.

O. I feel like a blind man led by a seeing dog. But is it that bad? No; I am not that blind and the dog cannot see that well. What I can see is that the fetus can feel something and can have certain sensations, perhaps even certain thoughts, because the nuclei of sensations, thinking and so on, are already there in a biological way. If you take a cell and touch it, then the cell contracts and defends itself by a secret war against the impression from outside. If a protoplasm can already defend itself that much, then certainly it is possible for the fetus to feel and to have a certain defence. I am reminded of the work of Ferenczi who compared the fetus in the water with the biological development of life on earth. That is exactly what I think Dr. Bion meant, but that was described already by Ferenczi.

B. My surgical chief, when I was a medical student, was Wilfred Trotter who wrote "The Instincts of the Herd in Peace and War". He drew attention to something which seems to exist. For example, take a group like this: We have a combined wisdom which is extraneous to the little that each one of us knows, but by analogy we are like individual cell bodies in the domain which is bordered by our skins. I think there is something by which this combined wisdom makes itself felt to a great number of people at the same time. We like to think that our ideas are our personal property, but unless we can make our contribution available to the rest of the group there is no chance of mobilizing the collective wisdom of the group which could lead to further progress and development.

There are certain highly intelligent people who cannot stand the perpetual bombardment of thoughts and feelings and ideas which come from all over the place, including from inside themselves. So they cancel their order for the newspapers; they withdraw their number from the telephone book; they draw the blinds and try as far as possible to achieve the kind of situation in which they are free from further impact. So the community loses the contribution that individual can make and the individual mentally dies—in the same way that certain cells in the body necrose.

The body has the intelligence to resist an invasion of foreign bodies like bacteria — or even plants, cocci — and mobilizes phagocytes to deal with these invading objects. Is it possible that we can organize ourselves into communities, institutions in order to defend ourselves against the invasion of ideas which come from outer space, and also from inner space? The individual is frightened of even permitting the existence of speculative imaginations of his own; he is afraid of what would happen if anybody else noticed those imaginative speculations and tried to get rid of him on the grounds of his being a disturbing influence. Freud quotes a drama by Hebbel about the sort of person who disturbs the sleep of the world and is hated accordingly; he came to the conclusion that he was one of them. When I was a psychiatrist in the British Army I was rash enough to suggest that the psychiatrists were administering drugs to their patients in order to have an undisturbed night.

O. It is still done.

B. I can well believe it — it has a great tradition, a great past and, I suspect, a very promising future.

Q. Aren't there certain interpretations which serve the same purpose?

B. Yes, exactly. Freud talks about a 'paramnesia' as being an invention which is intended to fill the space where a fact ought to be. But is one right to assume that a paramnesia is an activity which is peculiar only to patients and to pathological existence? I think psychoanalysis could be a way of blocking the gap of our ignorance about ourselves, although my impression is that it is more. We can produce a fine structure of theory in the hope that it will block up the hole for ever so that we shall never need to learn anything more about ourselves either as people or organizations.

Q. Would you elaborate on that? Most of us have built our professions round the extension of knowledge. Now you suggest that the methods we are using and our endeavours are to block our search for knowledge: I would like to know how.

B. I suggest that we cannot be sure that these theories, which are so convenient and which make us — both as individuals and as a group — feel better because they appear to make an inroad into this enormous area of ignorance, are therefore final. One would like to say, "Thus far and no further", but if one carries on this same procedure then one is back again in contact with this vast area of ignorance.

With care we can learn the laws of chemistry and physics and feel that *now* we know how the physical world operates; *now* we know the truth. But in fact the area in which the sort of physics and chemistry which we can comprehend applies, is extremely limited. Astronomers have discovered what they call a 'black hole' to which the laws of physics and chemistry do not apply. Indeed, the way in which the universe works is beyond our comprehension. Why not? We are ephemeral creatures; our little earth circles round an ordinary sun at the relatively leisurely speed of twenty-two miles a second. No one can imagine the rate of circulation of a spiral nebula around its centre although it is given a comforting and convincingly scientific appearance by saying that the rate of circulation of this spiral nebula, of which our sun is a part, has a diameter of something like 2×10^8 million light years.*

Q. Are you then asking whether we are any more aware of scientific usefulness in terms of the state of man's knowledge of the mind? In other words, we are at the point of transition.

B. I am impressed by the short, precise and exact diagnosis which is summed up by saying "Homo sapiens". It is a self-inflicted decoration.

Q. Do you mean that we fill our lack of knowledge or uncertainty with a kind of codified meta-psychology?

B. I would say so.

O. Theodore Reich used to tell us about what he called "the courage not to understand". And, in spite of all the remarkably complex and meaningful theories that you yourself have developed in your writings, you are aware, and want us to be aware, of how limited our understanding is. If we can cope with that, and help our patients to cope with that, we are indeed accomplishing a great deal and that is a great part of psycho-analysis.

B. I think it also helps to scale down our expectations of what we think we can do. Over and over again we measure our failures against a standard which is inappropriately high.

Q. Are you also saying that we are made in such a way that by nature we hate freedom? When you say we have to hate analysis because we are confronted with the patient who wears his id on the outside and the ego and super-ego tucked away, that we can't stand to be confronted with that, and if we were wiser we would follow the lead of the id —

B. No, but I suggest that somebody here should, instead of writing a book called "The Interpretation of Dreams", write a book called "The Interpretation of Facts", translating them into dream language — not just as a perverse exercise, but in order to get a two-way traffic.

Q. Is thinking so painful to us because we do not have the courage to face the limits of what there is to be understood by it?

B. No, I think it is because 'thinking' is a new function of living matter. I do not want to suggest though that some plants have no minds, because we don't know what sort of mind a vegetable mind is — for example, Venus's Fly Trap (Muscipula).

*see also p. 10

THREE

B. I want to stress an on-going question which seems to me to be of the greatest importance. By 'on-going question' I mean that it has no permanent answer; it is always open.

It is a good thing for an analyst to ask himself from time to time why he is doing analysis and whether he means to be doing it tomorrow and the day after that and so on. One gets into a habit of taking it for granted that one has decided to be an analyst, to be one for life as if it were a closed question; whereas I think it is important that it should remain an open question. [In analytic practice the precise instance of the general question is afforded by the decision to continue or to stop an analysis.]

The emergence of this problem requires careful thought by the analyst as to how he is to broach it to the analysand; only he can tell what language to talk and how to formulate, "What do you come for?", "What do you expect?", "What do you think I am going to do?" There are numerous answers: The patient has been advised to come, or recommended to you, or heard about you. It doesn't tell you a thing; it is a superficial reply. But there remains the open-ended question—why has this patient, who has come to you for three years, four years, five years, three weeks or three sessions, come again today? You may have an idea why he came to you yesterday, but that is not today. You can have a constantly changing opinion under the impact of the experience which goes on happening; therefore to treat it as if it were a closed subject does not leave room for development.

Q. Would you go as far as to ask the question, "What am I getting out of this analysis for me?—never mind an outsider."

B. Everybody goes that distance anyway. We don't like to admit it because it doesn't sound altogether respectable to say, for example, that I am here because I get something out of it; or I am an analyst because so far it has seemed to be rewarding. But basically one *has* to consider this. If you are practising medicine you may, like John Hunter, expose yourself to infection with disastrous results. In analysis how wise is one to expose oneself to this emotional experience? Am I going to have a breakdown as the result of the emotional force to which I am exposing myself by setting up as an analyst? Shall I be robust, healthy enough to be able to stand the strain?

Q. What about the other side of that? Is there anything curative for the doctor who helps the patient?

B. There is no chance of knowing that unless the doctor allows himself to be aware that he is concerned with what *he* gets out of it. He may have an urge to be helpful to his fellow men. In that case he does get something out of being a doctor and running the risk of catching the complaints. But he may not appreciate that that is a necessary component and is, therefore, subjected to that powerful emotional situation without having considered whether he wants to help anybody. This is putting it in extreme terms; it is never as clear cut as that. In time something begins to impinge; you become aware of some dis-satisfaction; the dis-satisfaction accumulates and has no outlet.

O. For a number of years Kleinian theory was not acceptable to many circles in New York City. Now there is a lot of acceptance, but there is considerable conflict in psycho-analytic techniques; the more classical group adheres, or has until very recently, to a much stricter definition of the transference; they don't make the same kind of early interpretations; they are less in touch with psychic processes. I wondered if you would share with us some of your thoughts on these differences.

B. I have not been particularly aware of differing from any other analyst. I *have* been aware of not knowing as much about psycho-analysis as I would like; that is brought home to me both in talking with another analyst and comparing his ideas with mine, and also by my patients who constantly demonstrate that I don't know a great deal of the subject. But this is not in any way different from any other kind of human suffering; people learn that it is painful to continue to live; they have anxieties of all kinds and they want some assistance. A great number of people go so far as to get married without considering what they mean to get out of it——

O. This goes for Kleinians as well as Freudians ——

B. I think so — it is easy to say, "I'm married". You can get a licence, you can get the State to support you in this idea. In analysis you can call yourself "a Kleinian" or "a Freudian"; whether it means anything is another matter.

O. Your uncertainty is reflective of what we all feel many times. But in psycho-analytic literature we are often struck by the kind of certainty which is almost foreign to our personal experience; references to the breast, the penis, the penis inside the mother, and all the kinds of things that don't sound nearly as uncertain as you do right now.

3

B. You have to try to make clear what you are talking about. A definition which avoids being vague becomes dogmatic; it is a matter of judgment. If a patient says to me, "I don't know what you mean", I say, "If you assume that I don't mean what I say, the problem arises as to what I *do* mean". To answer the question by a further elaboration risks distortion of what I, as analyst, have said as clearly as I could.

O. There is something I am struggling to understand—your notion that the analyst empty himself of memory and desire. One way I do understand it is in terms of trying to make myself as receptive as possible to what the patient is trying to communicate to me, but in terms of the way I work it seems to me that my own memories and desires play an important part in my understanding of what my patients are saying to me. I feel that I am caught up in a paradox.

B. [In this respect I agree with you: It is to avoid the distortion of the effects of one's own past history that analysts are supposed to be analysed. In practice it means that one 'consciously' attempts to exclude one's memories, hence rid oneself of memory; for the same reason one needs 'consciously' to exclude desire. When we have not been analysed, or are tired, the obtrusion of memories and desires becomes a liability.] The more one is occupied with what one wants to happen and with what happened, or what one knows about the patient or psycho-analysis, the less space is left for uncertainty. If I become more and more dogmatic, and more and more sure that the patient said this, that or the other to me last time, I know I must be getting tired. When we are tired we find it difficult to be receptive. The actor has to learn to articulate so that he is audible at the beginning *and* at the end of a performance: The analyst has to be receptive and sensitive at the end of the session as well as at the beginning.

It is easy to fall into the comfortable feeling that one knows a great deal about the subject and that the patient thinks so too; it is a contract which is made. I am reminded of a rhyme about two famous Oxford historians — Freeman and Stubbs:

> *Stubbs butters Freeman, Freeman butters Stubbs,*
> *Each ladling butter from his respective tub.*

O. I thought, as you were talking, that what matters to the patient is that his 'self' has to come to life, has to be augmented and expressed, so that by this emptying out of expectations and memories the analyst leaves room for the patient.

B. That is so. A patient may say, "I had a terrifying dream last night". This is said so quickly that it almost passes notice. "Terrifying" dreams, "terrifying" experiences—we hear it over and over again. But if you are sensitive you may begin to feel that there is something about it which is beyond just an ordinary statement. There are feelings which patients themselves slide over; they don't want to tell you how terrified they are and how unpleasant it is. If they do get to the point of admitting that, the chances are that they will say, "I was all right until I came to see you, but since then I have been terrified; I get frightened of almost anything I have to do". Of course you are not trying to frighten the patient; but you are trying to make him aware of the fact that he has that feeling of terror. A certain type of patient slides over many remarks inviting you not to pay attention to them and agreeing that they have made progress, are so much better. The next thing you hear is that the patient has committed suicide. The feelings have been of such intensity that while passing off the phrase "I had a terrifying dream" he does not allow you or himself to know how appalling these feelings are.

What do you see when the patient comes into your room? Usually a mature individual, articulate and much like everybody else: The patient sees much the same. He has heard this psycho-analytic jargon anyway and has got used to the fact that it doesn't mean a thing. So he naturally assumes that the analyst does not mean what he says. But the analyst has to be aware that the patient *does* mean what he says, although he may say it very softly indeed. We should not allow ourselves to be too dominated by the noise that the patient makes— "When I was coming here today I saw an accident in the street........". That is perfectly true, but the noisy way that spectacle can be described by the patient makes it difficult to hear these other noises which are not being made so clearly. [It is the 'forgotten' — 'unconscious', 'repressed' but nonetheless active experience which has been re-awoken by the immediate stimulus of the accident; at the same time the immediate experience has been reinforced by the 'forgotten' element.]

So — you have to have your senses wide open to all kinds of hidden characteristics. Most people don't see what is the matter with a colourless person, but a doctor ought to be able to see that this indicates an anaemic condition. There is something about the colourlessness of the patient which is more than ordinary everyday pallor. This applies equally to what the analyst sees and hears of the patient.

O. There is a difference in the Kleinian culture; maybe interpretations are more cryptic or more related to your own perception than hooking into what is happening from the patient. A certain orientation may put a slant on your interpretations.

B. Of course it does. That is one reason why I say it is necessary to denude oneself of memory and desire.

O. The Kleinians say that one uses one's own phantasy therapeutically— one's own counter-transference reaction, all of one's reactions to the patient, and some kind of unconscious communication between the patient and the analyst.

B. I am very happy that the Kleinians do that; if that is what they like doing that's fine by me. But it is no good to me.

Q. Could you tell us about yourself then — how you work?

B. I am doing so.

O. You mentioned to me recently that when you and Melanie Klein were involved together you made quite a strong condition that you were your own person when it came to thinking and reacting— that this was a very important condition in establishing relationship.

B. Yes; she said she was prepared to agree, to put up with it. I don't think this was particulary acceptable because she wanted to make it clear that when she said the infant evacuates parts of its personality it doesn't want and shoves them into another person she meant just that. She did not want it supposed that that was not her opinion. There is the dilemma: She had to be dogmatic enough tc say, "That is my opinion; it is an omnipotent phantasy". But I don't feel that what I am exposed to in my office is just a phantasy of the patient's. There can be millions of rational explanations; the patient can say things which are so exasperating that you get annoyed and angry. That could be said to be splitting off their feelings of hostility and putting them into the analyst. But perhaps it is not so simple as that; perhaps something really takes place when two people are so closely associated as they are in a psycho-analytic experience. If these elements don't exist what is the good of doing psycho-analysis anyway? If we are simply conversing like anybody else, why call it a psycho-analysis? Why put up with years of sessions about nothing in particular? There must be some reality corresponding to this 'meaningless' term 'psycho-analysis'. It is just an invention; a verbal noise — but I think it has been invented because something exists which has to be given a name.

Q. On the one hand there is something steadfast about the description you are providing of yourself in working with the patient despite what you call an open and emptied mind. On the other hand there is a notion of some kind of change or growth that takes place in you along with the patient. Would you comment about that

apparent contradiction? My other question is, can you see yourself
learning about counter-transference reaction from your patients?

B. Taking your second question first: My understanding of the
correct meaning of the term 'counter-transference' is that it is
unconscious;* since it is unconscious the analyst does not know what
it is. So I have to put up with the fact; it is to be hoped that I am
aware that I have there elements about which I can do nothing unless
I go to an analyst myself and get them dealt with. It is a question
of making the best of a bad job. The bad job happens to be me. I cannot get thoroughly analysed — I don't think there is such a thing.
It has to stop some day; after that I have to make the best I can of
who I am.

   In answer to your first question: Supposing we were really steadfast, one would wonder what was the matter with us. Time passes, we
grow older, and if our ideas remain the same there must be something wrong. It is much more likely that we fail to notice the change
that is taking place in us; the actual work that we do, whether it is
organizing a shop, or being a doctor or surgeon or analyst, has an
effect on us. It may not be at all clear what it is. When you were
young, grown-ups said, "How you have grown!"; they stood you
against the wall, marked the height, and there! There's proof that you
had grown. But if the child is in fact 'growing up' we cannot stand
that personality against the wall and mark its growth.

O. I had the impression from a seminar of Donald Meltzer's I once
attended that Melanie Klein gave off interpretative remarks almost
constantly, and that these were in the order of ruminations — she
ruminated out loud.

B. I would not have called them ruminations, but I think that she did
give a constant stream of interpretations. Latterly I would have
thought that they were too coloured by a wish to defend the accuracy
of her theories so that she lost sight of the fact that what she was
supposed to be doing was interpreting the phenomenon with which
she was presented.

Q. You have observed the patient; he is there in the room with you;
you have some impression; you must make the decision to communicate it or keep it to yourself. How do you deal with that
question?

B. I have to act 'on the spur of the moment' as we call it; you are
spurred by the moment. You decide not to say what you think you
observe, and the patient doesn't turn up again. Or you *do* say it and

*see also p. 16

the patient thinks, "I'm not going to a person who tells me these alarmist stories; of course he wants me to come for an analysis; of course he has a vested interest in making money out of patients, and naturally he would tell me I need an analysis". So, on the spur of the moment you have to react. It would be surprising indeed if you felt that your reaction did not leave a great deal to be desired.

Q. Is it always an obstruction if the analyst, in addition to having an impression, thinks conceptually about the ego state, the state of resistances, the degree of symbiosis or individuation that this patient is marching towards in terms of libido— and so on? Do you see these primarily as concepts that obscure and fool us into thinking that we know more than we do? Or are these working hypotheses ever of value?

B. I think they are quite useful for about three sessions— if you are lucky enough to see the patient on three successive occasions. You know nothing whatever about the patient and therefore have to formulate some sort of theoretical opinion — the theories in that instance taking the place of facts, because there are no facts. After that you hope not to allow your theoretical preoccupations to obscure the impressions to which you should be exposing yourself. This is not easy to do— there would be something seriously wrong with your patient if he couldn't make a fool of you. At the same time there is something seriously wrong with the analyst who cannot allow himself to be made a fool of; if you can tolerate it, if you can tolerate being angry, then you may learn something. Never mind about all these theories of what analysts *ought* to be; what we ought to be is a matter of no importance in the *practice* of psycho-analysis or in the practice of any part of real life. It does matter what we are.

O. I am disturbed about the issue concerning counter-transference. In the last fifteen or twenty years some of us have come to realize that what used to be something that one was to consider himself guilty for experiencing and acting out with a patient, is a human experience that occurs in the patient-therapist relationship related to the therapist's past. In *Second Thoughts* I noted that you referred to counter-transference a number of times as if you believe in it as a theoretical concept. What I want to get to now is process rather than theory. If I react strongly to a patient I may, after reflection, feel that I over-reacted and ask myself, "Who does this patient remind me of? I seem to be allergic to something in our relationship that is triggered in my being with her at this moment and I then intellectually, through memory and feeling and other associations, realize that in some way she does indeed remind me of my sister from an earlier period of my life." Ordinarily I would then conclude that I have been experiencing a counter-transferential reaction and have displayed some evidence of this in my over-reaction — or what I now believe to have been an over-reaction. What seemed to have been helpful to me I might — or might not — then share with my patient, depending on how appropriate I felt it to be. This I label my 'counter-transference' and perhaps might then use it more openly in the future in my work with this patient. You say this is an unconscious experience which, because it is unconscious as it occurs, is therefore unavailable and not particularly of value; in a sense you discard it. I am troubled by that.

B. I would say that while you are with the patient there is nothing you can do about it. But, thanks to what you have been saying, when you consider the matter afterwards you can decide — and this I do think is possible — that your reaction was something which would fall into the category of counter-transference. In that way you have a chance of learning something about *you* — it is one of the 'fringe benefits' of being an analyst.

O. I am interested in your concept of the container which fits into some of the different views of counter-transference. The previous questioner was talking about the more classical view of counter-transference, something from our own past that we transfer onto the patient. I think the Kleinian view is that the patient induces in us certain reactions; good and bad aspects of the self are split off and projected into the analyst, and the analyst is thereby induced into feeling and behaving in certain ways. Many analysts are totally unaware of the kind of counter-transference the Kleinians talk about. Some of the newer concepts of counter-transference are useless. Instead of sitting there and suffering and getting angry with the patient it would be viewed as a way of actually boring the analyst, dehumanizing the analyst, deadening the analyst, keeping him at a distance. The reaction of the analyst can be used in a therapeutic way; in fact some of the modern thinkers in psycho-analysis feel that the counter-transference may be the most valuable thing in the analysis; they feel that the negative therapeutic reaction comes out of this kind of negative counter-transference more than any other factor in analysis.

B. If it doesn't come into analysis there is something wrong with analysis. We are extremely dangerous animals; of all the ferocious animals that inhabit this earth the human being has succeeded in killing off all rivals — except the virus. At the end of the First World War the 'flu epidemic killed off far more people than had been killed in the war. For all our wonderful destructiveness we are nothing like as efficient as the virus.

In the analytic session one is concerned with two dangerous and ferocious animals, one of whom— and possibly both— has at the same time a wish to be friendly and helpful to the other. Parents retain an impulse to continue to be helpful to their children even after they have sent them off to earn their own living. In the analytic situation we are not usually dealing with a blood relation but with a mind which is very like our own. I think one is under an obligation to remain civilized, but remaining civilized is not the same thing as being unaware of what human character is really like. We are concerned with powerful impulses which are anything but civilized — murder, hate, love, rivalry. So we have to be sensitive and aware of the powerful emotional nature of the two objects in the same room at the same time — as well as this element which wants to be helpful. Even the hostile patient would like to be helpful to the analyst and turn the analysis into an everlasting one so that he doesn't have to find any more friends— he just sticks to the one in the office.

We are faced with a paradox; we are struggling both to retain such civilized capacity as we are capable of and at the same time to make evident the primitive and dangerous nature of the situation.

Q. If you were too civilized might you be destroyed by the patient?

B. Yes. Translanting Kant's statement * into the kind of thing we are familiar with, the individual is intuitive but doesn't match it with any concepts. If Kleinians theory has anything to do with the real facts infants must be marvellous Kleinians because they know all about what it *feels* like, but they have no concepts, they cannot write any of these great books— their concepts are blind. Later on they have forgotten what it is like to feel terrified; they pick up these words but the words are empty – "I'm terrified". You have to notice that it is an empty phrase, it is a concept; it is only verbal; the intuition is missing. If we can draw attention to this fact then possibly the *concept* of terror and the *feeling* could be married. The analytic procedure is an attempt to introduce the patient to who he is, because whether he likes it or not that is a marriage which is going to last as long as he lives. When the patient talks about terror he really knows what he is talking about. It is useless for the analyst to talk about some psycho-analytic theory unless he can say, "*This* is it".]

O. You said every infant is a Kleinian: I wondered if it is also true to say that every Kleinian is an infant.

B. Yes, absolutely — but unfortunately grown-up, and they look exactly like adults. We all have this illusion that we are adults, we have reached the peak, and have nothing more to learn. That is why I

*see pp. 25, 26

suggest asking this question which is open-ended — Why am I doing analysis?

O. I want to offer an assertion and ask your opinion of it. I have come to the conclusion that one of the analytic myths that we tell our students is the incognito of the analyst. I think such a thing does not exist. I had a discussion some time ago with a colleague; I said, "Everyone knows that the patient is plugged into the analyst, but to the same extent the analyst is plugged into the patient". In other words, the patient knows as much about the analyst as the analyst knows about the patient. Of course the difference lies in what each of them does with it; the concepts of transference and counter-transference are gimmicks which help us to conceptualize something, but are no help beyond that.

B.* [I am materially in agreement. I would not, however, describe transference and counter-transference as 'gimmicks' but concepts formulating illuminating observations which Freud made. It is the reality behind those concepts with which we, who practise, have to work.]

O. I have been thinking of your work, *Experiences in Groups*; I wondered if I saw happening right here in this room the dependence assumption. Everyone was saying, "Teach us; show us; you know; your thinking, your brilliance" ——

B. Not to mention the pressure to believe one is equally brilliant oneself.

O. Yes, as well as the audience. But what happens in reaction to the frustration when the dependence assumption isn't gratified?

O. I wasn't sure whether you were answering questions or making interpretations.

B. They are all interpretations of impressions; an impression which I get, which I expose myself to and then translate into verbal terms. But in this respect I am dependent on my sensory apparatus and on my capacity to interpret what my senses tell me.

O. I also felt you were interpreting instead of answering our questions. I was wondering whether this is the way you actually function with a patient, using your own perceptions ——

O. Like the use of yourself as the diamond that receives and reflects back.†

*The reply seems to have been irrelevant and has therefore been excised.

†see p. 15

Q. Is your discussion about the embryo in fact a discussion of where we are?

B. Analogically one can say that psycho-analysis itself is at its birth, so we don't know much about it or this peculiar, unpredictable development— growing up. That can be unpleasant; even the analyst can feel, "I don't like being aware of this universe in which I live". After the First World War everybody decided that the Western Powers had won and that now we were in for a very good time — all would be well. Santayana wrote that the Great War was not an aberration from which we had now got back to normal happiness and good health, but that it was an hors d'oeuvres which ushered in the return to the normal state of affairs—fighting, destruction, rivalry, hatred.

Q. You have often said there is so much about analysis that we don't understand; I have the same feeling. Would you tell us about a current case in which you feel you don't know what is going on; what you are doing with it or thinking about it; how you are trying to understand it?

B. The patient said, "I had an awful dream; I dreamed I was swimming and I suddenly discovered that the stream was carrying me straight through a weir; I was going to get sucked in and destroyed. I tell you I never woke up so quick in my life." That is a curious statement. Ordinarily you would think that if you were swimming and found yourself in that situation you would get out of the stream. But it is peculiar to say that this is such a terrifying dream that "I tell you, I never woke up so quick in my life". It takes some sorting out because it is not the way in which I am used to talking, and it is not the way in which I am used to thinking either. The extraordinary thing is that this particular patient has always succeeded in earning a living and has been married and had a family. So there must be something which is right about it; there must be something about that way of thinking which I don't understand but which must be useful. I would like to know what it is. I have thought about that plenty of times — I am not much nearer to understanding it.

There are other stituations which are similar. It is difficult to communicate to you the factual situation. The patient said—as near as I can reproduce it— "I'm awful. I got through these exams, but I don't know a thing about it — not a thing." That was about the end of the facts. The rest of the session was taken up in a conversation which would appear to be a link between the patient and myself because we were using ordinary words. But there was no idea of who the patient was, and no idea of who I was — only the link in between. That is a queer conversation; that is a conversation in which — putting it into mathematical terms — there are plus signs, minus signs, signs intending to mean division, division of X by Y, but no mention of what X and Y are or what the two sums are that are to be added or subtracted.

Q. Are you saying that you couldn't tell from the patient's conversation why he said these things to you?

B. I had no idea. First of all I would want to know what the language was — it's not mathematics. It appears to be American or English; it *appears* to be, but it isn't. I could say it is a matter of semantics; it is not. I could say this is a language in which a sentence is composed of conjunctions only. But this conversation does seem to have an effect; the patient keeps on coming to the sessions and I continue to agree to see him. But how that is brought about I do not know. I said to the patient, "You haven't yet told my why you come here". "I haven't told you why I come here? I am doing nothing but" says the patient. I can only assume that the patient is correct; why it has passed me by I do not know.

Q. How does the patient react to learning from you that you haven't the foggiest notion why he is there despite his belief that he has made repeated efforts so to communicate? What does that do to the patient to learn that you are confused?

B. [If the patient had 'learned that I was confused' they would not have been listening to what I said. "I do not know" is not the same as "I am confused". I might be confused or angry or frightened, but those are private matters which I consider to be irrelevant. I do not mind the patient 'analysing' me, but in fact he has come to be analysed. It is important if *he* is confused or angry or frightened, and it is important that I should make him aware of that. It is wasting his time to tell him what my troubles might be — those are matters for myself and my analyst.]

Q. Do you think the patient doesn't want you to know what is going on?

B. I think the patient wants me to know and expects me to know. I am obtruding an irrelevancy if I behave as if I do not understand what he means as if I were irritated or bored. The trouble is that I am frightened of being ignorant of what is going on.

Q. To come back to the statement of the patient, "I got through the exam but I've no idea how". I take it from what you said that you didn't do anything with that statement; what followed was a senseless or not understood dialogue. Was it based on that statement? Or did you ignore the statement? Did the statement do anything to you?

B. I drew attention to the fact that the patient was not talking a language I understood; therefore I was not receiving the communication.

Q. You did not make an attempt to get what was behind that message?

B. Yes, I did, because it seemed to me to be a highly dangerous situation.

Q. And in a case like this you would not follow the traditional procedure of analysis and ask the patient for associations to it?

B. Yes, as soon as I am tired I do exactly that. I say, "Thank God for the accepted procedure".

Q. I would like to clarify what you said about the 'evidence' for the truth of an interpretation.

B. I am prepared to accept the theory which scientists put forward about this. It is what I call 'apodeictic' proof, facts which are inescapable. They are forced upon you; something happens which forces you to accept it as the proof of the previous controversial matter. However, this is complicated by Heisenberg's Uncertainty Principle. If the physicists cannot say what a fact is, then this ignorance and the disappearance of certainty is liable to spread.

O. I had in mind the experience where there is a sudden evidence of the truth.

B. Yes, something convinces us that what has been said is illuminating.* But what that is a proof of is another matter. I don't think one can say that it has much to do with facts except facts about the human animal as it is now; there are certain experiences we have which carry conviction.

Q. In *Learning from Experience* you talk about thought disorder and about modifying an experience rather than thinking. Does that tie in with the description you gave of the patient who was talking on and on and you couldn't find the link?

B. The link, I am convinced, is not articulate speech; it is something else. Sooner or later someone who is exposed to the experience I have been talking about may be able to formulate this peculiar kind of 'umbilical cord' as a method of communication between the two people. I could say that this type of conversation is like a breast which might connect an infant with a thing which turns out to have a mother stuck on the other end of it, so the breast and the mouth come together. That is all very well as analogy, as a pictorial image of

*see p. 13 Prince Andrei, *War and Peace*

what is going on, but what is the 'thing' that is going on? If one could climb down the DNA helix to a point in infancy, perhaps one would be able to know. But if one climbs up and reaches the same point, only on a different level on the helix, what is it this time when there is no mouth, no breast, but this peculiar conversation which is nevertheless effective? Since the patient is talking to me and using his language I ought to be able to be receptive to it; I ought to be capable of hearing this communication and of knowing that the patient has told me what they come for. As the patient says, why don't I know?

Q. Couldn't you be effective just by your presence, by being a container or a battery charger?

B. Possibly. Why does one have to know? I feel pressure to know because I think it is dangerous not to. I may be in trouble if I cannot understand what the connection is between somebody or something not me and what I consider to be me.

O. Winnicott talks about the analytic situation which is similar to transitional objects where the omnipotent phantasy of the child is reinforced by the responsiveness of the mother. It is the responsiveness of the analyst trying to know what the patient wants, of the experience of somebody being tuned in to him, that is unique to the analytic situation for many patients.

B. This is a useful idea if you are old enough and intelligent enough to be able to talk English in that kind of way. If the patient is falling back on a method of awareness which was available when he was an embryo being communicated with through a watery medium, then it may be obvious to the patient *how* there is a contact—but not so to me. It is important to be aware that the relationship between the two things — the patient and myself — is only transitional, a transient experience. It is as well to consider that a word like 'transference' has shades of meaning which are applicable, like 'transience'; it is only temporary, the moment at which the two paths cross for a short space of time during which a method of communication is employed by the patient which I am able to receive but do not know how it is done. I would, however, like to be able to verbalize it; I would like to be able to put it into some language — painting, music or mathematics.

[The patient that I described as saying that he had got through an exam but did not know how, showed by his constant repetition of that state of mind that the important matter was not conveyed by the ordinary meaning of the words, but was conveyed by the monotonous reiteration. In short, I can only describe it as a 'musical' contribution. That 'music' eventually became clear to me and I was able to give him an interpretation of what it was that he was conveying.]

FOUR

O. I have been thinking about the opportunity I had with a patient who came back after seventeen years. I got a call; she asked me whether I remembered her — I really didn't, but I remembered the name. The thing I have been pondering is that this lady told me that for all these seventeen years she had been holding on to something I had said; it was a kind of magic. What interested me was that I don't think I ever said it; it doesn't sound like me at all. It was, "There is no law that you have to stand in line with his bullet." I may have talked about her relationship to her sadistic husband, that she had the right not to take the kind of sadism she was expected to, but it was the wording that interested me — I don't think it was mine. There was such gratitude and magic in this. She returned because she hoped I could again come forth with a phrase for this poor suffering soul. She had had an awful life. A child of hers had been killed by a fall in an elevator shaft—partly due to her husband's carelessness in leaving doors open in his own factory; and her older son died of a horrible cancer. The first time I saw her, her first words were, "I have a few little problems", and out came this horrendous account. It was Dr. Bion's speaking about language as a communication which interested me; you don't often have a patient coming back and telling you what they think happened. Did I say it unconsciously? Did she hear something, or did she make this up? How does one know? Or doesn't it matter?

B. We all have to get used to an extraordinary thing; this queer conversation, which we call psycho-analysis, works — it is unbelievable, but it does. The result is that you give various interpretations which you may or may not remember. It is difficult to believe that you may nevertheless have sown an idea which has germinated and given birth to still other ideas until the patient comes back and tells you ideas which she thinks — and probably quite rightly — she got from you. But you don't recognize them because you haven't seen what has happened since you sowed that particular seed in her mind. If you had a son or daughter who went away for seventeen years you might be surprised at the physical resemblance that person had to yourself and take a moment or two before you realized that in fact it was your son or daughter — similarly with ideas. So I wouldn't in any case be particularly disturbed by the discovery that some idea

46

sown during that previous contact has germinated and come out in the form she can recognize; after all, it has grown in her and not in you.

[What matters is that a patient establishes the psycho-analytic ritual of so many sessions a week, so many weeks a year and so on. The origin of the ritual may be difficult to trace; thus peculiarly distressing circumstances, about which nothing can be done, are a fruitful source of omnipotence, omniscience and omnifascience. So, it is likely that this patient would want to believe that the analyst was a beneficent power which she could adore; this would required interpretation. The analyst could fall into the mistake of accepting the proffered omnipotence, or alternatively of ignoring the *fact* of the help she had given. Patients do not come back for nothing. The analyst has to establish what is relevant and what is not. This implies a standard of Truth. In practice truth can only truly be described as an aspiration which may be beyond the capacity of the human mind.]

Q. Could you elaborate on a distinction you made between 'good and bad' and 'good and evil'?

B. [The Nazi ability to organize the Nuremburg rallies was 'good'; the use to which it was put is a matter of opinion. In my opinion it was 'evil'. It is important for the patient to know what is *his* opinion. To conceptualize the difference would require an ability to discriminate between the moral and the technical.]

Q. I have re-read your paper on *Memory and Desire*. In it you say the psycho-analyst should forget the patient has a past and a future in relationship to him. I don't think you mean that as concretely and specifically as it is stated in that paper. Could you elaborate further on that?

B. I have to use this new-fangled trick of human speech which is only a few thousand years old; I have to use words which are extremely crude and exaggerated, black and white. As far as the meaning is concerned they are not only black and white; they are often so fuzzy it is hardly possible to make sense out of them. We try to pull this faculty in the direction of doing something for which it is not intended, namely, the investigation of the human mind. So we put forward these statements and hope that the individual reader will be able to turn them into sense of some practical kind.

Q. Could you give an example in clinical practice of how one can suspend memory in working with a patient? Is there a technical device for that?

B. When I feel a pressure — for example, "I'd better get prepared in case you ask me some questions" — I say, "To hell with it; I'm not going to look up this stuff in Freud or anywhere else, or even in my past statement—I'll put up with it". But of course I am asking you to put up with it too— an impromptu affair of this sort.

With regard to your patient you could say, "Surely I ought to look up the notes on this case. Oughtn't I to have made some notes on what this patient said to me? What would happen if the patient ran me into court for malpractice on the grounds that I hadn't prepared notes, that I didn't even remember what I had said before?" I can well see that you would get an unfortunate experience out of trying to explain in a court of law that you had not in fact done it because you don't think it works very well. It is much easier to believe that you don't do it because it is so nice to be lazy, not to worry with these things, to enjoy life instead. It is, oddly enough, difficult *not* to do; I should be very surprised indeed if, towards the end of the day or week, anybody resisted the pressure to drag up some psycho-analytic theory rather than go on not having the faintest idea of what the patient is saying or doing. But tomorrow is not today; and if tomorrow is seventeen years later—as we have just heard—we may not even recognize the face of the patient or what the patient said, and feel guilty about being greeted as if we had done something helpful. Unfortunately we tend to feel that our ideas aren't worth preserving so we are liable to lose touch with them. The patient who returned after so many years may have discovered that what you had to say was a great deal more valuable than you realized.

Q. Does it matter whether I said it or not?

B. It is hard to say. We think it matters whether we analyse people or not; whether it *is* worth doing is a different matter. The spoken word certainly seems to be powerful. Tacitus gives a description of the behaviour of the bards amongst the German tribes who used to recite to the tribe, and from its reaction they would tell whether it was safe to proceed to war or not. The function of the bard could be called diagnostic; the function of the leader can be to try his seductive songs of war or murder on his audience. But does this mean that it is of use for us to talk to other people about 'the self'? It would be of considerable use if we could mobilize a meeting on the scale of the Nuremburg rallies; it seems to me that we have to assess this matter of the efficacy of human speech against the background of history so far.

Q. When the child or the patient evacuates does a vestige remain? I am thinking of the infant who cries—feeling unpleasure or hunger— evacuating into the mother. I cannot imagine that child losing that feeling of unpleasure.

B. Partly because the evacuation takes longer than is supposed. In other words, the child has to do what it 'thinks' is an evacuation — it has got rid of these nasty feelings and ideas. [The 'vestige' remains, but has a power like that of a wound which festers.]

I get the impression that even the person who has dealt with the problem in that way has a feeling that something has taken place which must be kept out. So, once you have got rid of the unpleasant feeling, idea, proto-idea, primordial idea, keep it out. It doesn't seem to be far from what Freud said, that the repressed has to be kept repressed, except that I would reinforce this now by saying, the 'evacuated' has to be kept evacuated; it has never been unconscious. Some different word from 'repressed' or 'suppressed' is required for elements in the mind which have never been conscious *at any time* — and that means they have never been unconscious either.

Q. Would the term 'non-conscious' do?

B. If you find the term 'non-conscious' serves your purpose I certainly think you should retain it in your vocabulary. I find it easier to consider the existence of thoughts without a thinker. It has been put rather differently by Pirandello as the title of a play — *Six Characters in Search of an Author*. But why stop at that? Why should it not be something which is even smaller, more fragmentary than that? It is a thought wandering around for some thinker to lodge itself in.

Q. You don't want old language, you would rather find things without connotations?

B. I have tried to use them in this way: There can be certain things which we would nowadays call thoughts or ideas but which are really physical. I am dubious about using terms like 'the adrenals' and 'the optic thalamus' when I am talking about the mind. I shall never know whether there is any such thing or not, but I think it is convenient to leave one or two boxes empty in case somebody is able to fill them up. Similarly with regard to these diagnoses which are floating around — leave them unattached till somebody pulls them down to marry them with their proper origin.

O. You used the word 'evacuation' first as a kind of synonym of projective identification; later it appeared to depart slightly from the meaning of that term. I wondered if you could draw a distinction between the two. To me it seems that evacuation is a much more radical process than projective identification.

B. It is more radical because it is more concrete. But as soon as one starts giving words a more concrete meaning they become even more distorted. Or you can leave it up in the stratosphere of intellectualization — 'projective identification'. Melanie Klein herself said it was a bad name — it is.

O. Hanna Segal said that you have explained it pretty well and applied it clinically more than anyone else.

B. It may be because of the advantage of being analysed by Melanie Klein and having the experience of being told, "You are doing it".

Q. What is the difference between identification and projective identification?

B. ['Identification' should be kept to mean what Freud said it meant. Similarly, 'projective identification' should be kept for occasions when the occasion itself — as observed by the analyst — seems to fit in with an interpretation which the analyst thinks is better expressed by Melanie Klein than it would be by words of his own.]
    The fetus has no choice but to get born, and is forced out into harsh gaseous fluid instead of a nice watery fluid. And similarly we have no choice except to communicate our interpretations by virtue of the gas — air — which we use or abuse for phonation.

Q. Is water always better than gas?

B. Not always, because the fetus is clever enough to take a little of the watery fluid in the nasal channels. The result is that it is still able to breathe and to smell. Smell travels very well in a watery fluid; it is a long-distance receptor. Fish can smell decaying matter from a distance of many miles.

Q. Do you think the fetus can smell in the womb?

B. Yes, but that is an imaginative conjecture; I have no evidence for which I could claim a scientist's validity.

Q. Obviously the question of language is a very difficult one. But if we are going to discourage the use of words hitherto familiar but already empty of meaning, how are we to talk to each other.

B. I cannot see any alternative to disagreement and discussion amongst psycho-analysts who know what the problem is to which they want to draw attention.

O. I would like to germinate the idea of thought without a thinker. I thought of Lewis Carroll who dealt with this concept easily; The Cheshire Cat — the smile without the cat. Then I thought of Edward Lear — wonderful so-called 'nonsense' poetry which might have more sense than any other poetry because it has its own unfilled language. I feel that Doctor Bion too wants to make this unfilled language and

I can sympathize. I have great doubts of how much can be used of the existing language and the habit of human thinking. I think a two-and-a-half or three-year old can be better analysed than an obsessive intellectual adult who has every word defined and comes to analysis to learn about himself. I find that kind of very bright patient particularly hard to deal with. Are there people you deal with who still have a balanced enough mind to think new thoughts? What do you do with this idea of thoughts without thinkers?

B. If they were our thoughts we might be able to do something about them. But since I am trying to define the possibility of thoughts *without* a thinker, I am talking about things which are not within my capacity and which may not yet have found a lodgment in me.

[The importance of the last speaker's comments cannot be exaggerated. Her own example may save the child from the worst excesses of the modern 'Babel'; the child analyst's position is onerous and exciting.]

O. We have two polarities: At birth the possibility of germination and the possibility that we can have a baby; then we have all these images of catastrophe, war, storms and terror. This seems to be the implication you are making.

B. You can regard birth and death as being extremely important, but they are not diseases. Nevertheless there is such a thing as maternal mortality; there is such a thing as infant mortality; and there is such a thing as death for people who are old. The result is that these apparent conjunctions make people think that they are therefore syn-onymous. It is important that one should see a distinction. Of course that itself is a slanted view, a view that we should learn how to talk articulate speech. *Our* concern is with the interval between birth and death and the need to know how to use articulate speech in our work.

O. There is a phrase that I read in a paper by you about the psychotic and non-psychotic aspects of the personality that has intrigued me. I have never seen it used anywhere else and I don't think you explained it at great length in the paper; it was "the furniture of dreams".

B. [We 'furnish' dreams with what we remember as pictorial images. What they really are will have to be determined by practising analysts.] It is true; one is always leaving these loose ends for the simple reason that one knows so little and one's life is so limited. Even mental capacity fades too fast to be able to carry these things through. One hopes that some phrase of the kind you mention can turn out, in the hands of somebody else, to achieve a meaning which could be useful.

O. Almost like a thought in search of a thinker.

B. Yes. But where did you get that idea? You could try to label the owner, the originator, the creator, but I think you would soon find you could not. For all you know it may even be you; you can be the storm centre of your own storm. You may be originating something without being aware of the fact. This survival from the past about possessions — my this, my that, my idea — seems to me to be nonsensical, although I can well understand why someone like Melanie Klein can be irritated if she finds that the ideas or theories she produced are debased and devalued. One would like to have some respect for the ideas and keep them in their original bright working order. To do that you may have to invent the language you have to speak while you are speaking it.

Q. And hope to be understood?

B. I think that is being a bit greedy. The luxury of hoping means that you have first of all to hope that you have not been talking nonsense and that there is somebody else who is able to make sense of it. In this respect we are almost like cell bodies ourselves; there could be an idea floating around without a lodging place, without having found an appropriate cell sufficiently distorted for it to lodge in.

O. Children in play therapy, finding something is painful, frequently feel it has something to do with the air. They may blow bubbles, make aeroplanes.

B. I suppose children's games are fun for a time, but then the children begin to quarrel or get bored — which I think is the same thing as getting frightened. What is frightening about a game of fathers and mothers with dolls? As analysts we begin to suspect that these games are not 'just games'.

The child goes off to the mother or father and says, "What shall I do now? I can't think of anything to do" — the game has become intolerable. Later on, when individuals are not playing fathers and mothers but are actually being parents, they have forgotten the fun element and so this 'game' becomes so terrifying an occupation that they want to rush off to God or Devil or Psycho-analyst and say, "What game shall I play now?" What game are they to play if the thing which is not in fact a game at all, but which might have been both the real thing *and* fun, hasn't worked out?

The fact that people can say "this is not working out" means that there is some hope for it; perhaps something better is being found. But so long as people draw a well-patterned coverlet over the games they get on with underneath, they will dislike having the coverlet removed.

I don't think we can be sure that people won't get so frightened that they say, "Let's have it all back again -it may be humbug, it may be lying, it may be deceit, but at least it is more comfortable than this factual world you are inviting us to face".

Q. What about the reality of *our* group at the moment? How is everyone reacting? What is happening here under the coverlet?

O. I don't feel all that terrible emotion some people are hinting at. I think Doctor Bion is extremely demanding of us and I find that very stimulating.

O. I feel a sense of dissatisfaction and restlessness.

O. I feel fascinated.

O. I think one of the feelings of uneasiness is connected with language. We are talking in the tradition of German/American/ English. This afternoon I was reading a paper by a French analyst and this evening I was thinking how psycho-analytic theories must feel different in different languages. We, as Americans, do not have the investment in our words that French people have; we have a different way of talking to each other and of talking about the things we experience with our patients. I am wondering if a lot of the unease has to do with shifting into completely different gears. We are used to talking a kind of shorthand to each other and there is something about the proceedings here which is reminding us that we are talking shorthand.

O. I recall at the conference at Topeka in 1976 on Borderline Disorders the contrast between the way in which psycho-analysis was talked about by the European analysts and the American analysts. It seemed to me that American psycho-analysis is more akin to baseball than it is to European psycho-analysis.

O. Yes, we are not philosophic, poetical, historical; we are more technical. That is the way we are used to talking to each other.

O. That may be a fault.

B. It is possible that the genuine Americans still retain an experience of what it is like to live in a strange and dangerous world in which warmth and food are not obviously forthcoming unless you produce them. In that way you can have it forcibly brought home to you that even the matter of food is not to be taken for granted unless somebody does some work for it. Although you succeed in being so successful that living becomes comfortable — houses, central heating, electricity and so on —there can remain a rooted remnant of awareness of the fact that life is not really like that. It can look almost like a kind of schizophrenia: On the one hand you have a culture, a capacity for thought, which has lost and forgotten the primitive base; on the other hand there is this remnant, vestige of an awareness of the reality of things. That seems to me to produce something which is as near to a synthesis as to become noticeable. You produce wonderful physicists, chemists, Nobel prize winners, but there remains that highly active vestige — roughness, violence. In Europe it broke out; there had to be a 'Great War' to make people aware of these thick layers of hypocrisy which are difficult to penetrate without a most painful birth process. [This discussion here is the prototype of what American civilization might do to make the violence — of which we are all aware — redundant.]

Today there may be some quarrel going on between the 'thinking' done by the body and that done at the cranial end. There is some hope that in spite of the fact that we all have diaphragms they are not purely non-permeable membranes; we hope that they do move up and down and do in fact have a lot to do with continued life. So maybe there is something analogous to mental movement by which the two are mingled. The representative of a trade union suddenly discovers the charms of being the boss and becomes 'cultured' — but what culture is that? Does he then become completely divorced from these 'inferior, lower class' people who work with their hands? One hopes that the diaphragm will be more likely to mingle the two than to cut them in two halves that do not rejoin. The situation requires more than a conjuror or his tricks. As analysts we try to elaborate a technique for ministering to a mind diseased, razing out the rooted trouble; it is an unpopular occupation. [Being analyst or analysand is hard; no one who is not robust need apply. It is not safe to be unaware of the danger.]

O. The term 'projective identification' implies the continuing contact between one and the other. Evacuation does not imply that.

B. Melanie Klein said that patients *think* they evacuate something: that they have the *phantasy* that they have got rid of this chunk of themselves into the breast or the mother, although it only sounds like words, the sort of thing you puff out of your mouth. If a chimpanzee shows its hostility by making a rude noise with its lips it can have an effect on the baby chimpanzee it is trying to silence. The question is, to what do you attach importance — the flatus, the gaseous flatus you evacuate through your lips, or the noise you make in doing so? When does cacophony turn into music? When do these rude noises which you make with the aid of instruments like bassoons and tubas — and even with your mouth — become beautiful music?

Or wonderful ideas? When do rude noises masquerade as profound thoughts?

O. It sounds as if the distinction has something to do with the nature of the product. Projective identification always implied to me a product that had more completeness, wholeness and structure than the fragments you talk about as 'bizarre objects'.

B. There is a great advantage in its having some material quality. You can say, "black man" or "white man": there you are: you don't have to do any further thinking; they have arrived completely coloured and correctly labelled. So why waste time going through all this fatigue and nonsense about thinking about him or her or it or them? Why not deal with it according to the colour which has so mercifully been provided so one can tell which is which without thinking?

O. The point is, how you feel about 'black'; how you feel about 'white'; and what kind of emotional reactions we have for the black and white. I will try at the same time that I attack you to defend you too. You are talking in general about no-man's land — which of course is true. We don't know what a thought is; we can describe it, but we don't *know* it. That is what you are doing all the time. But if we want to talk about what affect it has or what impact it has, to use it in a practical way, then we have to do it somewhat differently. From time to time I can grasp what you are saying; I think there could be an original idea. And then you talk on with almost dissociated ideas, making big jumps — what we are thinking, or what goes on in the universe or the atmosphere — and then I get lost. Until all of a sudden you make an excellent remark and something could come out of it — and then I get lost again.

O. That is what Doctor Bion attempts to do. I don't blame him for not being more clear because in essence nobody can be more clear about the things we discuss.

B. I agree with you. One of the few situations in which we can defend ourselves is when we can say that what we feel is a *fact*; I think it is about as near to a fact as we are likely to get. The patient can say, "I know for a fact what it feels like to be me, and to feel what I feel when I sit in this room with others or by myself. That I know; that I am satisfied is a fact. All the rest of it is theory — psycho-analytic theories, French theories, English theories, black theories, white theories, any colour you like to mention". It is awkward if a Newton says that 'white light' is really made up of a number of colours. There's an intellectualization for you!

Q. That bastardizes the feeling of black and white — it makes everything more complicated and confused?

B. Certainly. If you say that that black person, or that white person is in fact a human being, that really mucks up the whole thing; that means that somebody has to do some thinking. You are thrown back on this horrible occupation of thinking.

O. You haven't talked about the Grid.

B. As soon as I had got the Grid out of my system I could see how inadequate it is. ["He put in his thumb and pulled out a plum, And said 'What a good boy am I!' "* But the satisfaction does not last for long. As a pictorial model I suggest the boy sucking his thumb, pulling it out of his mouth to examine it with admiration, but in time becoming dissatisfied. What I experience is that 'theme with variations'.]

Q. Is it not workable?

B. [It is for you to decide whether it is any use to *you*. If it is not, do not waste time on it. The same advice applies to any future Grid that I might formulate.]

Q. Is it hard?

B. Not for me— only a waste of time because it doesn't really correspond with the facts I am likely to meet.

Q. How does Melanie Klein's theory of envy as an inborn attribute help us to understand the earliest development of the infant?

B. It probably helps you thanks to the intervention of Elliott Jaques. Having read the book he said to Melanie, "You've got the title wrong— it ought to be 'Envy *and Gratitude*' ". That she had left out. That book is meaningless unless one also detects the gratitude.

Q. How is it helpful to think about this as a preconception, as something which is innate as opposed to something which is learned?

B. We can use beta-elements and alpha-elements in order to talk, or to provoke an argument or a train of thought. But before I can translate these bodily sensations into an idea I have to retain some capacity to understand the language my body talks to me. I don't like it because it so often misinforms me. I dislike having things done to me which don't cause me any particular harm but which are

*nursery rhyme – *Little Jack Horner*

appallingly painful. So I would like to get some assistance from the cerebral end of my body which would translate that into a language which was more useful, more comprehensible and more to the point. Assuming that I have to be prey to the body I was born with and to what it persists in telling me, before I can attempt to be articulate and to aspire to these heights of highly intelligent theories I first have to go through all kinds of unpleasant stages. One of them is what I would call speculative imagination or speculative reason. Unfortunately one has to go through this stage when one is extremely vulnerable; someone may say, "What rubbish you talk! You have imagined it". True — or dreamed it in a lucky frame of mind. But if one then, under the provocation of being contradicted, says, "It is not just imagination; it is a fact", that is not accurate. The appropriate child of a speculative imagination or speculative reason is a *probability*. The mathematicians think they have formulated a theory of probability. That is not a fact; it is only probable. Somebody who knows some mathematics may be able, thanks to their analytic flair, to elaborate a mathematical theory of probability which is some use.

Q. There must be some use for this idea of inborn envy. How have you found it of use either in the understanding of the infant and the interaction with the mother, or in some way understanding what the patient is going through?

B. A patient to whom I had been giving a prolonged period of interpretations was furious and burst out in expressions of violent envy and hostility whenever I said something which appeared to be a gratifying discovery about him. I said, "There is one person in this room at any rate who is really envious of you, and that is you. When I was rash enough to say that that was a very interesting observation you had made, there was at once a great burst of vituperation, both against me for saying such a thing, and against yourself for having said something which excited attention."

Q. How did the patient react to that?

B. After a time he began to become more tolerable and tolerant. This patient could only wear clothes of a certain colour — no departure from that particular optical wavelength. He had learned to tolerate some clothes enough for purposes of survival provided he stuck to the same clothes which he wore year after year.

Q. What makes that innate?

B. I don't know. I would be inclined to say that somebody's ovum and somebody's spermatozoa had got together and had an inter-

course which produced an object which has these striking characteristics. By the time it succeeds in getting born — and hasn't so far
at any rate committed murder — there is one person whom nobody
can save and that is the patient from himself. If he wants to murder
anybody he is the one victim who is always available at any hour of
day or night, and no analyst or parent can intervene between himself
and his Self.

FIVE

Q. How do you use the term 'caesura'?

B. I would like to have an idea of what this area is which is being
delimited when you say "caesura". I was saying just now that I think
I can feel when I am in what I call a "capital city" and that I feel
New York is one. I don't care what the map says or what is said by
any other place; that is not what I am talking about. I wouldn't like
to try to say what a capital city is. So when you ask me about the
caesura — and indeed any of these words we use — every one of us
needs to be aware of this thing which is the *origin* of the sensation
that there is something around. When I say there is something
around which I would call a 'capital city' it is no good suggesting I
should go and look up the words in a dictionary or a guide book.
There is no guide book to the domain or area we are talking about.
What then is the 'capital city' of this caesura? What is the core of that?
I have been asked this question, but I am trying to put to you that I
cannot really tell you because I don't know how it is to be verbalized.
Perhaps between us all we might be able to find an approximation to
it, some method of indicating the focal point, the focus of a conic
section. But that is again only another model; people have tried to
give it various names like 'spirit', 'soul', 'super-soul', 'id', 'ego'; they
none of them get me very far.

O. Maybe a colloquial reference, 'where it's at', is as good as
anything.

B. Yes. A phrase like that conveys something to me. This is what we
are up against the whole time: How is this awareness to be communicated to somebody else? Where does this communication start,

where is its origin, where or how is it initiated? Did the place initiate the feeling that it is a capital city, or did the idea or some primordial thing, and a whole lot of those primordial things getting together, produce something for which the name 'capital city' had to be found? It is not the bricks and mortar, but the people in it; then it isn't the people in it, it's the souls inside them. This is the sort of issue you are up against in tomorrow's session.

Q. Is it primordial? If we find a realization which a capital city is it necessarily localized in individuals?

B. I don't think it is so at all. I think it is convenient if it obtrudes to a point where even we notice it. But that is not because I am blind and have only just seen the bricks and mortar. It is something else which obtrudes which makes me feel there is a pressure which I find hard to localize.

If you show a dog a photograph of a little boy it smells it, realizes it can't eat it and that's that. But put the same thing on a movie and project it onto a screen—then the dog gets excited. It is only a photograph but it is a moving photograph and that the dog begins to think has a meaning. We also; there are certain things which set up a vibration. Then we begin to notice something. So if we allow ourselves to be sufficiently sensitive for long enough then we shall begin to feel something impinging on us. We might ultimately find some way of communicating it.

Q. Is psycho-analysis a depth phenomenology?

B. There is a lot to be said for a phrase which was used by Melanie Klein to me; "Psycho-analysis is a meaningless term, but it is available." It is a word in search of a meaning; a thought waiting for a thinker; a concept waiting for a content.

O. It has had many contents.

B. Unfortunately that is true. There is no shortage of material available for mental nourishment, but what the unfortunate mind is stuffed full of we don't know. The amount of rubbish which is lying around for purposes of filling a space is enormous. Freud talks about amnesia as being something which fills a space when you have forgotten what belongs to it. That would be all right if I knew where the pathological ended and the genuine began. It is nice to think, "Ah, psycho-analysis is *it*; that's what we all need." Do we? Or is it more stuffing? Is it more noises to occupy an empty space? This point can only be decided by those of us who are engaged on that activity we call psycho-analysis for want of a better word.

Poets have found a method of communication: Milton invents a word, 'pandemonium'; Shakespeare strings together ordinary words in a way that starts things vibrating inside countless generations of people. Why? How is it done?

Q. Are you suggesting that not only do we need to invent the language but we need to be more poetic in writing about the things we discuss?

B. No. I think the central point is that you need to dare to be available to something you want to express; to dare to allow a thought without a thinker to lodge somewhere in the range of your capacity. It might be to make marks on paper; it might be to make marks on stone; or it might be the capacity to set electro-magnetic waves moving. In other words, a person writes a bassoon concerto; if somebody else is clever enough to be able to play the bassoon and translate various black marks on white paper into sound waves, then that communication spreads if there is anybody around prepared to listen. The artist is dependent on the off-chance that someone will listen or dare to turn himself into a receptor. The patient is dependent on the analyst being sensitive to the faint signals which he cannot make louder. But in turning ourselves into receptors we are taking a big risk. From what we know of the universe we live in some of the information may be most unwelcome; the sound or signal we receive may not be of the kind that we want to interpret, to diagnose, to try to pierce through to this 'thing' behind. [A real poet is able to use language that is penetrating and durable. I would like to be able to use language that did the same.]

O. I am interested in the process of communication or dialogue, or lack of it, which goes on in this group. I have a feeling that maybe you want to make us continuously realize what it feels like when there is no communication between us and you. But whatever you say is always fascinating; I'm not sorry I came; it's nice to listen. I am simply hurt, insulted that you offer us dialogue and we don't have dialogue. You let us know — and I know that anyway — the shortcomings of language, the dangers of feeling concepts prematurely, the necessity to leave the characters wandering alone before we conceptualize, define. But nevertheless human language isn't that bad; you cannot think it is that bad — you write a lot and we all enjoy reading it. So you certainly know how to use language. Today someone threw in the idea of 'caesura'—without aggression, without asking for a definition, just to play around with it. But you didn't react to it; you play around with the idea of why one cannot define anything. I wouldn't mind if you had come and said, "Let's have no dialogue; I'll just talk". That's fine too; I love to listen to you.

B. It is unfortunate that in the situation you describe, instead of being able to develop the possibility, my own personality obtruded. [If you are right the dialogue has been spoiled by me, and you are right to feel that it could be better done by somebody else.] I try to give you a chance to fill the gap left by me. Perhaps tomorrow in our sessions each one of us may be able to learn something which I have *not* been able to tell you.

O. It seems to me that what happens in this room is something which happens in our offices with equanimity with certain patients. We do not gratify their questions; we give them something they can use which is — as you were saying earlier — planting the seed for germination. I particularly appreciate that you are not so explicit because it gives me a chance to get in on my own thinking and my own development.

O. Everybody is interested but there is some strange wish to mystify things for which human language would be adequate.

O. I have a different feeling — although I have felt exasperated at times too by not being able to focus in the way I wished. The sense I am getting from Doctor Bion is that he is so aware of how concepts can be misused and concretized and become part of the luggage that gets in the way, that in justice he misreads his own concepts which many of us have found very useful. We might misuse them, true —

O. He doesn't suggest that you misuse them; he suggests you might put them to better use than he does.

O. Yes, but if we try to deal with any one concept, that concept is already no good.

O. It seems to me that Doctor Bion's purpose is to help us to think differently and that he doesn't feel that ordinary dialogue is useful.

O. If that is true then we shouldn't be asked to ask questions. Let's say we just sit here and listen to whatever Doctor Bion says — but don't ask any questions.

O. Then he won't be able to have his effect.

B. I plead that by my actual presence I am behaving as if I did think there was something to be said for dialogue and even for getting together, conversing if possible. But at the same time I don't want to mislead you into supposing that my characteristics, whatever they are, are therefore necessarily desirable. You may indeed have to overcome that particular hurdle in order to get to the real truth behind it.

The central thing is this: In my experience there is a real truth behind this debate; although I have not got there myself, somebody else may. Plato's dialogues have provoked thought amongst people who weren't even in existence when he originally engaged in them.

O. In the last few days I have thought back to some splits that have come out and have been troubled over them —I have not been so stimulated in a very, very long time. Maybe we are just expressing the pain of being made to think.

B. There is a certain redeeming quality about it all; we can still retain a hope that somebody, some time — perhaps now —will do better than our Selves. I know my limitations up to a point. There are plenty of opportunities for me to learn about all my faults and mistakes; they are uninteresting, and they are a nuisance. Nevertheless one hopes, somewhat optimistically, that in any given community there will be people who can do better. If you have a family of your own you hope that it at least will avoid most of the blunders the parents have made.

O. I am a bit mystified by something that I sense going on amongst the group. I don't understand everybody's readiness to agree that we are non-thinking people. As a group we have talked to each other about exciting ideas over tea, over meetings, before patient, after patients till midnight. We are not stultified, ironclad; I don't know what kind of model we are setting up to say we shouldn't be.

O. I would like to take it back to the beginning, to my question about the caesura. I think Doctor Bion answered my question very well. It was taken out of context; it was an idea that occurred to me after the discussion about intra-uterine existence and the problems of the fetus.* I was wondering what Doctor Bion meant by caesura in that context. I have no complaint about the way he answered this question. Perhaps now that we understand that this was good enough we can go on from there.

Q. Don't you think that many of us feel a great deal of frustration?

O. I don't like anybody to speak for me. I find Doctor Bion most inspiring and I think I understood some things. So I have no quarrel at all with the way he handled it.

B. My difficulty is that I have to borrow words from the past; but the past is finished, there's nothing we can do about it —

O. We can understand it —

*pp. 27, 28

B. But I have to use that vocabulary and unfortunately, as you rightly remark, we understand it. What I am trying to point out is something we *don't* understand. I am going to use this model, but I want to warn you that it is only a model and it is liable to obscure more than it illuminates.

There is such a thing as the birth of an idea; I suggest that it is a most uncomfortable experience. Whether it is a group of people or an individual which is giving birth to an idea the pains which are associated with that experience are extremely upsetting and disturbing, and somebody will certainly try to put a stop to it; nobody likes pain. I think it would be rash to assume that this problem is only within this room. We feel that the individual is unique and deserves to be given a chance to blossom, to grow, to develop, and for there to be a space in which to do that — whether it is an individual person surrounded by a skin, or whether it is an idea which is much more difficult to recognize. I should be surprised — again falling back on anatomy and physiology — if the phagocytes do not collect and try to gobble up this new idea before it gets more troublesome, before it turns into a contagion or an infection. It may not be a pathological idea and its destruction could therefore be unfortunate. That seems to be the magnitude of the problem which faces each person here or in the office. We can consider and debate these matters; it would be a great pity if we didn't dare to do so. Physicists and chemists can draw this wonderful diagram of the DNA molecule but they have not defined the difference between the animate and the inanimate. *We* are sure that there is one. A table seems to be different from the things that we are. Defining it may be a matter of little importance but I am sure that there are feelings, embryonic ideas, primordial ideas which deserve to have a chance of development. I do not know whether they will turn out to be good or bad; somebody has to have the courage to say, "Even if the child I give birth to is a monster I'll risk it".

O. It would require a very strong person.

B. Yes, and there may be little willingness to admit the strength of such a person. It can be assumed that anybody can give birth to a child or to an idea—it's so easy. Then there's trouble when you find it isn't easy. I see no reason, for example, for believing that the psychoanalytic movement will not be stamped out at any time by government, an authority, something which has power behind it. But I don't see why we should therefore be intimidated and refrain from psychoanalysis.

O. I think we have many phagocytes in this city that are always, as you point out, gathering to make sure that a still-birth occurs. It is difficult under those circumstances to produce an idea that is not only new but which will survive long enough to become threatening.

B. I talk about white blood cells, using this pictorial language —it is a verbal form of pictorial imagery. There are people who are impatient of the restraints of verbal communication and find other methods. Valéry said that it is assumed that the poet is a person who is undisciplined, disordered, goes into a rhapsodic state and emerges, wakes up with a poem complete in his mind as the outcome of an undisciplined, intoxicated — literally and metaphorically — state of mind. Valéry believed that, on the contrary, the poet is much nearer to an algebraic mathematician than to an intoxicated individual.

O. Coleridge would say, "Weave a circle round him thrice..."*

B. These issues are involved in seeing your patient tomorrow —the one that you haven't seen so far. Even if it is one you think you saw anatomically yesterday or last week or last year, it is not the one you see tomorrow.

O. Could you give us some hint as to how we could see that patient in a way we haven't seen him before; how to suspend any memory of having had contact with that patient. I have been attempting to do that and it is very difficult. The patient's name is in my appointment book so I can't eradicate it from my future unless I am going to do away with my appointment book.

B. It is indeed difficult to say how to denude one's mind of pre-conceptions, memories and desires which make such a noise that one cannot hear the patient speak —at least not the one that we need to hear speak. In my experience the noise of my past has so many echoes and reverberations that it is difficult to know whether I am really listening to the patient or being distracted by one of these ghosts of the past. I have had the experience of seeing a young adolescent and thinking to myself, "It's very queer; he hardly says anything, but he sits there with that silly grin on his face". I couldn't think what it reminded me of. The next morning when I was shaving I saw it in the mirror —that's why it was so familiar. This young man was supposed to be an adolescent; he wasn't supposed to be the analyst; he wasn't supposed to be teaching me anything. I was supposed to be analysing him. But in fact he had held a mirror in which I could see my face – but I didn't recognize it.

Q. What did it teach you about the adolescent?

B. It taught me that I had better try to forget these painfully

*Samuel Taylor Coleridge, *Kubla Khan*

acquired ideas about psychiatry, psycho-analysis, psycho-therapy and the rest of the luggage which I was carting around with me; it interfered. If I had only been able to see at the time I might have been able to make some contribution which was helpful.

Q. Like what?

B. I don't know — I never made it. I lost the patient at the first interview — and he was quite right.

Q. If you could speculate, if you had understood what you understood next day, what might you have done?

B. I can't say because I cannot now draw upon the actual information which I might have been able to use at the time had I been open to what was being made available by this patient. In other words, the analytic session is priceless; the potentiality of the analytic session, the direct emotional experience is out of reach almost as far as value is concerned. What other people are prepared to tell you about the patient is worthless compared with what the patient tells you — maybe verbally, maybe dramatically, maybe mimetically.

O. What you are saying then is that you capture the thing-in-itself by isolating it in the analytic session. But it seems to me to be very difficult to be able to capture the thing-in-itself if you don't have the necessary training.

B. That is one of the big difficulties. As Freud put it, you have to know where to look, where the apparition will appear — literally. I am not talking about a ghost; the thing that appears does appear. You need to have your senses directed towards it. Then when you begin to feel something you might close in and focus on the point of irritation — using the term in the neurological sense of nerve irritation.
    [J. M. Barrie led his audience to expect the appearance of Mary Rose at a stage entrance towards which the whole cast directed its gaze. By this means the actress was enabled to enter unobserved. With the raising of the lights came the illusion that a spirit —not a physical body —had been present.]

O. It seems to me that this 'baggage' we bring with us is akin to a character-honouring that prevents a kind of neuro-perception.

B. Yes, it is possible.

O. It can be baggage that interferes with communication, or it can be wisdom that facilitates it and magnifies the possiblity of having an experience. You can't say that theory is baggage——

5

B. No, but it turns into baggage. My wife asked me, "What shall we take to New York?" —

O. You had very little luggage!

B. "The temperature is 80 today — yesterday it was 40. Which lot shall we take?" You see; it is as simple as that. But when it comes to a question of mental baggage, that really is a problem. I believe that on the whole the kind of psycho-analytic baggage I have collected is more of an asset than a liability; what is left by the time I have mobilized it seems to be more valuable than what I have discarded or what I have forgotten. But only time can tell; unfortunately it is unlikely that we shall live long enough to know the truth.

O. While with a patient my mind wandered briefly to a personal preoccupation. The patient said he felt disconnected. I don't think I had made a sound but I know his feeling was related to my thinking about myself. I don't understand it.

B. The impression I get is that this is a fundamental, primordial characteristic. I don't think it is acquired through reading books or meeting people or having a lot of experience of life. Even the infant is aware of feelings of dependence *and* isolation. Grammatically there is no difficulty in describing it — "I was all alone in the room with so-and-so". But we attach very little importance to those words. It is only on looking at it more closely, only if you bring to bear our psycho-analytic microscope, that it turns out that that commonplace phrase has a meaning that most people aren't aware of. I think you can be stirred to the depths by something which seems to be so insignificant that it is hardly noticeable; it is probably lost in depths of knowledge so that this spark of insight gets swallowed up.

Q. Is there an association between your recommendation that one eschew memory and desire, and the notion of abstinence that Freud used as applied to the analyst?

B. I would have thought that they are fairly closely associated. Melanie Klein used to say she wasn't a 'Kleinian' analyst, she was just a psycho-analyst working along the same lines as Freud. But whether she liked it or not she was condemned to be a 'Kleinian'. So, with reference to your question, one would like to be able to acknowledge one's indebtedness without insulting the person from whom one says one has borrowed the idea.

O. The other similarity I thought I saw was in the recommendations that Freud makes in *The Interpretation of Dreams* of how one should approach the dream without preconceptions.

B. That is so; I don't think it is distorting what he said. We hope to quieten down our internal noises so as to hear what is being said. It is difficult to combine this with the use of knowledge or experience which other people have made available. It is the difference between actually living life and theorising about it.

O. When we live life we also feel that—I think Kant was right—we cannot know the thing-in-itself. There is always something in human perception which is already there. Children say, "We cannot crawl out of our bag". We try at least to crawl out as much as we can, but only if we keep in mind that we actually *cannot* shall we get relatively as close as possible. One questioner sounded as if he would have taken you literally, not as a façon de parler, saying "if I look at my appointment book I know the name, I know who the patient is". Of course one has memory; of course if I go from here to there I have a theory of laws of motion. One cannot do anything without an implied theory. We might want to talk metaphorically to give an intense feeling, or we might want to spell it out. But we shall be a little closer to knowing the thing-in-itself if we point out that we cannot know it.

B. One has to dare to go through various preliminary stages before one reaches even a theory. That is what I meant when I talked about daring to exercise your speculative imagination and your speculative reason; the place which one would like to occupy with facts is taken by probabilities—probability, using it in the sense I understand Kant to use it, as being something for which the facts are inadequate. It might turn into a fact later; there might be enough evidence to justify saying, "I know if for a fact". But what we have to deal with are situations which are stimulated literally on the spur of the moment.

O. We all live by our theories whether we know it or spell it out or not. Most of us live by the theory that ghosts or poltergeists are not around. I am aware of that because I have a patient at present for whom it is absolutely natural to believe that poltergeists exist. She is a daughter of a poltergeist-layer, so she grew up with the attitude, "Daddy has a poltergeist to day"; like, "Daddy has a new patient"—there will be money coming in. Her assumption is that if the curtain moves someone was here—no fright, nothing; just about the same theory as I expect this chair will not fly away. Maybe there are poltergeists; she might be right; it is a probability.

B. I can have theories about babies and even about what babies think, but babies don't have to have theories about it—they think. I can imagine—again indulging in speculative imagination—that at some point the baby begins to suspect that behind the food and the seat which carries it around there is an actual person. But there is no language for it; you have to wait before you call the thing "Mother" or "Father".

O. I always thought a baby called it an 'object'!

B. It probably did — if you could translate it back again into the original language.

Q. Why wouldn't the first experience of what is known be a 'being'? Psychic experience is non-sensuous — how could it be a 'thing'?

B. I can imagine noises of something rushing through my cranium, or thumps taking place somewhere inside; and I can imagine that I might be suspicious that some 'thing' had got inside me. The baby cannot make use of articulate speech so there is a big gap between the baby who knows the facts and we who know the language. One can identify oneself with the person who is potentially capable of articulate speech; one can also — or so it seems to me — retain some ghostly characteristics which know things unknown to me, but which are not verbalized. All that my body says is, "I've got a pain". It isn't very informative; it is not much more informative than somebody on the road using their horn — it doesn't tell you much. You cannot interpret that into movements of your feet and hands which will activate the clutch and brakes.

O. I would like you to say something about hate. You were talking about events prior to knowledge, on the way to being knowledge; I was confused because you said that events which are not yet knowledge are probable. And hate is something absolute.

B. [When I speak of 'absolute hate' I refer to one pole of love; there cannot be darkness without light.]

Q. In your article about the psychotic and non-psychotic parts of the personality you described the feeling of anxiety when your patient told you he was going to attack you. Could you describe that feeling? Is this a common occurrence?

B. It is quite common enough for me not to like it and common enough for me to have automatic methods of being aware of it. I do manage to keep in good working order an established defensive system. From that point of view I automatically defend myself against feelings and experiences and people who start stirring up some disagreeable feeling. At the same time I am also trying to understand what is going on. So one is at war with oneself in this respect; one is at war with one's natural defences.

Q. When you described the feeling in this article you said it was following your interpretation that this patient tried to put into you the fear of the attack; that the patient then clenched his fist so that you could see the whites of the knuckles. Did your interpretation make him angry?

B. Certainly. It is one reason why we would be somewhat optimistic to suppose that the analyst and the analysand did anything which exempted them from hating psycho-analysis. We are perpetually, by our own activity, stirring up the hatred of this occupation in both people. But we mutilate our Selves if we become incapable of feelings of hate as well as feelings of love. The problem is how to avoid auto-mutilation and at the same time not to mutilate these tender, growing shoots of civilized conduct.

O. I think all analysts wonder whether the development of psycho-analysis this century is a good thing for the world or not. It is so painful.

B. Yes, it is.

Q. Could you elaborate on what you said about analysts hating themselves as analysts?

B. There is no shortage of enemies — external and internal. So on the whole one regards it as redundant to create some more. All right — so far so good perhaps. But the next step is, when do we start defending ourselves and defending a position which we may not have decided is defensible — like standing up for psycho-analysis, maintaining the right to practise psycho-analysis before we have had a chance to make up our own minds in some really convincing way that we have supporting evidence for its value?

Q. How about defending the right to make up our own minds?

B. It's a nice idea; otherwise we would have to consider the possibility that our minds are made up for us by forces about which we know nothing. We do want to defend this idea; we do want to defend the occupation of trying to investigate our ability to make up our own minds.

O. I worked once with a psychotic patient who came to me when he was about thirty five; he had been in treatment since he was twenty. His greatest idée fixe was a sentence, "I am not homosexual"—and he wasn't. He could only work at night; in the daytime he couldn't be on the street. He worked in a kitchen in a nightclub and there he accumulated all the notes the waiters left around to make sure that he had not automatically written, "I am not homosexual". After many years he asked if he could bring me those notes — that was about fifteen years ago. He became better and started to have a normal life, worked during the day and started to talk to people. Altogether he became more alive and very circular in his phantasies. I suggested that maybe we could stop.

His other idée fixe was that he wanted to hold a woman in his arms; he wanted to be able to love a woman and be married. He said he knew he could grow and he did indeed become better and better. I blamed myself for having almost given up on this man.

When he was in his fifties he met a woman in his office, a divorcée with two sons, and fell in love. I couldn't believe it. I kept thinking, "Why did I think this man couldn't do it?" He married her and although he had never attempted sex with either man or woman, after a few weeks he functioned and loved it. They were married at Easter and planned to go to Italy for the summer.

When I came back from my summer vacation he didn't show up for his first session. I thought, "Ha, he is doing so well he is forgetting me — fine." The next session he didn't come. I called up his office. He had had a heart attack and died.

I wondered, did he work himself up to a way of life for which the frame, the machinery was absent? Does it matter that he died? He died with his widow surviving him, not like a homosexual, so maybe it was worthwhile. What was this whole story about? I don't know. Did he benefit from thirty five years of treatment.

Q. What you are saying is, did you kill him?

O. I wondered of course.

O. He did the growing and he did the dying.

Q. Did you think he would live for ever after you had cured him?

O. He was only fifty six when he died.

Q. Is it possible that he somehow linked love with death – when he blossomed in love he was closer to death?

O. The widow called me and said, "I know my husband saw you for a while before we got married". She added, "Fairy tales don't last long — it was a fairy tale, it was so beautiful".

B. I remember a primitive maori discussing a matter of this kind; he said, "Is man a stone that he should live for ever?" If people embark on this rash venture as animate objects then they are going to die.

O. I came to that conclusion too.

O. Maybe this is connected with the hatred of being an analyst. Most people have a pretty good idea of what they do or don't do in their work; we can never know.

Q. Your question is, did you help him, or did you help him to death?

O. Yes.

O. You can never know — which makes it rough.

Q. What difference does it make since death is a part of life?

O. True. He had a few very happy months.

Q. Would it have been better for him to live to be seventy?

B. I find myself struck by the toughness of what we call 'conscience'. It has been remarked, conscience makes cowards of us all*; so it does. It is one of the really vital bullies which is difficult to bring under any control. For one thing, it is so moral. Anybody who poses the free play of morality is by that very fact sinning. In certain religions people talk about 'original sin'; Freud talks about 'free-floating guilt'. It has a long history — long before anybody managed to attach an articulate label to it. So you can be reasonably sure that whether you are analysand or analyst you will be a prey to feelings of guilt and can even be set off on a career of crime detection. The individual can spend the whole of his life carrying out penitential exercises, devoting his attention to confessions of sins of one sort and another, and even committing crimes in order to have something to confess.

O. I guess I wanted to confess it.

B. It is a great sin for somebody to enjoy themselves. If he had a few months of happiness — and what is worse, sexual happiness — somebody would be sure to suffer for it; if nobody else, the analyst.

O. The confession helped — I have never told the story before.

Q. Would you say that the Catholic Church's doctrine of original sin is another way of people from past history talking about the burden of guilt that each of us is bound to assume, and that some of these people were just as wise as Freud in perceiving that?

B. The religious people generally have a long history of acquaintance with what is called the 'soul' or the 'spirit'. So it is not at all surprising that the remains of these various past histories are recorded in one form or another. Nor is it surprising that we find ourselves up against this same phenomenon, this same fact of guilt,

*'Conscience doth make cowards of us all' – Shakespeare, *Hamlet*

either experiencing it in oneself or seeing it operating in somebody else.

Q. Would we be human without guilt?

Q. But do we have to have so much?

O. It seems to me that it is more intense than a hundred years ago. The destructiveness we see rampant today is the other side of guilt feelings in terms of aggressive impulses. I am indulging in speculative imagination and just wonder if in the year 2000 or 3000 — assuming there is a world at that time — the phase of the human being will follow the present trend, or whether there can be some kind of change.

B. Couldn't we be vulnerable to the accusation that not only do we continue to exist but we also have aspirations to live a life worth living — which is adding insult to injury! If indeed we are guilty of this aggressive act of actually being animate I don't know who or what we are opposing. I see no reason for believing that the universe in which we find ourselves is friendly disposed. Locally, on our planet, animate objects exist. But the scientists, with their various space probes, have not yet discovered a sign of life anywhere else — although it is true that they have not even escaped from the solar system.

O. It is like the crime of being born human.

B. Or potentially 'civilized'.

Q. Why do I have such a depressed feeling now?

O. You remember Kurt Eissler's paper — he doesn't feel that the human animal will survive; man will destroy himself.

O. We shall become an extinct species.

O. It has happened before with many other species.

O. To revert to this stamping out of memory: I know what you mean, and I know you mean something good, but the danger is in taking it too literally. Physiological memory is the genes — they cannot be stamped out.

O. I took it as a metaphor.

O. Yes; but I think we should remember that the physiological memory is there; whether the original sin is there or not, whatever is there — the potential for joy too — we live by our physiological memory.

O. But when we are really absorbed in something we don't have memory.

B. I would like to invent a couple of words to get on with — 'genotypes' and 'genomenes'; meaning by the genomene the birth of a thing which appears, the counterpart of a phenomenon.

Q. A phenotype?

B. A phenotype and a phenomene as a counterpart to a gene.

Q. What does it mean?

B. I don't know — I invented it in the hope that something will come and nest in it; that some loose content which is floating around will find somewhere to lodge.

O. You invented this term in connection with memory and I am struggling to make a connection.

B. I suspect that there is some counterpart of the term 'birth of ideas'; that there is some reason to imagine that these painful experiences which we have are related to the process of giving birth to an idea — or "struggling to make a connection", which is an instance of thinking. An institution, a society of human beings may be unable to survive the birth pangs of an idea — it splits apart. We are undoubtedly careless with our psychological midwifery. We seem to feel that the thing to do with a newborn idea is to give it a good hard smack.

O. If ideas are pro order they have a good chance of being accepted. But if the idea announces that there isn't any order — only disorder — that's pretty horrible even if it is true.

O. The way I understand memory is that it is always a partial aspect of an experience. Forgetting, tossing memory aside, is tossing aside a partial aspect of the experience, but if it is really taken up into the totality then the memory is a living component of the aspect of the larger totality of experience. So this business of genes doesn't enter into it.

O. Didn't Freud say that dreaming is, amongst other things, a way of remembering? Memory has many faces.

B. I would like to suggest that if anybody recognizes the remains, remnants of a culture floating up in the conversation in their office it would be a good thing to drop your shovels and get out your camel hair brushes, and deal with it very carefully so as to delineate the civilization of which it is a remnant, a survival which has become uncovered. I gave the example of the situation where you get nothing but conjunctions with nothing to join them to.* The idea which ought to be conjoined by what is floating up in your office is missing.

O. I am bothered by what you said about guilt — that guilt is a terrible thing. I think the terrible thing is psychopathy. Thanks to guilt there is such a thing as conscience. Melanie Klein speaks of reparation for guilt; Winnicott, of the capacity for concern which comes from guilt. The great danger of what you refer to as 'lying' is that behind all misuse of language there is fundamental psychopathy.

O. You sound as if you are talking about Watergate.

O. No, I'm talking about life.

O. What about the notion of surplus repression in relation to surplus guilt? There is misplaced guilt, inappropriate guilt.

B. Guilt is such a nasty feeling; it hurts so much. And when something hurts you your tendency is to hurt it back again, scratch it out. If your skin starts irritating, scratch it — even if you run the risk of producing weals which are not much better than the original irritation. But somebody, sometime has to dare to investigate this horrible pain. What you are saying does involve the further investigation of the guilt; not saying it does not exist or is not painful, but going on looking at it. Then you might detect psychopathy. It does involve standing up to the guilt of which one is aware. The same thing happens with other emotions; it is no good talking about a brave man when he is avoiding being aware of the danger which he runs; he has to know it is a dangerous situation he is handling. What is known and felt to be dangerous and is still kept in view seems to me to be real bravery.

O. To be aware of the dangers of psycho-analysis and then to practise it —

B. And go on practising it.

O. It is either heroic or psychopathic!

O. I have always liked the statement of a wise analyst who said, "By the time you know why you got into the practice of psycho-analysis it is too late to get out."

*see pp. 42, 43

SÃO PAULO
1978

These talks, given in April 1978 under the auspices of the Sao Paulo Psycho-analytical Society, were the third of their kind and took place on consecutive evenings with a week-end break between numbers Five and Six. This is an edited version of spontaneous contributions made by Bion without written notes of any kind. I hope that, in spite of editing necessary for the printed word, I have preserved the essential freshness of his spoken communications.

ONE

B. I am not going to talk about psycho-analysis because I assume that everybody here is familiar with the analytic experience. I am convinced that there is no substitute for actually undergoing analysis with an analyst. People are often misled by the fact that we talk in the way which is familiar in ordinary conversation, so that technical psycho-analytic terms like 'Oedipus complex', 'projective identification', 'identification', have almost become part of cultivated speech; it is not understood that it is essential to undergo a psycho-analytic experience. Those who think that they know all the psycho-analytic jargon believe that they can talk just like a psycho-analyst to a patient who comes for help. But 'just like' is not the same thing as 'psycho-analysis'; the result is a great proliferation of different kinds of psycho-analysis, usually 'new and improved' — using those words sarcastically . That kind of treatment evokes a powerful, emotional situation and the so-called psycho-analyst reacts emotionally himself. The further immediate result is that psycho-analysis gradually gets a worse and worse reputation. If this process continues long enough psycho-analysis will not be able to survive. Thus we bear a heavy responsibility.

I propose to talk about the problems with which the psycho-analyst has to deal when he is psycho-analysing. Freud was impressed by the motto of Paris—"Fluctuat nec murgitur"—which he translated roughly as "Storm-tossed but not submerged". The person who is a good imitation of a psycho-analyst *is* submerged by the storm he evokes. The more desirable state is a difficult one which I will try to describe like this: The analyst, if he has had a real analysis and training by a real psycho-analytical institute, is a feeling person. So in this stormy turbulence he shares that emotional experience because he is a feeling person. He is also trained to think while admist these stormy emotions.

Using war as an example: An officer is not supposed to be unaware of a terrifying and dangerous situation; he is nevertheless supposed to be able to go on thinking if he finds himself in a position in which panic, panic fear arises — let me remind you of the god Pan. But he is not supposed to run away. He is supposed, in spite of being in the midst of this emotional storm, to go on thinking clearly. In that way he forms a focus from which the more disciplined reaction will build up; the troops will not run away, but will begin to stand fast.

I use that model deliberately because the situation in the consulting room appears to be so different. It is usually a comfortable room and apparently there is nothing to be frightened of. Yet patients can get up and leave the room and never come back again. The analyst is not supposed to find himself a prey to emotions which cause *him* to leave the room; he is not supposed to be unaware of these powerful feelings, nor is he supposed to stop thinking clearly. Nor is he supposed to be overwhelmed by desires, including sexual ones. This situation is basic, it is fundamental, and although it appears in groups it also appears when there are only two people in the room. One could very nearly express it in biophysical terms, such as the chemical products of the adrenal bodies. When do these chemical reactions become functional in the embryo? When could the embryo be said to feel fear or aggression? I am aware that we cannot hazard a guess without being vulnerable to the accusation that we are simply indulging our imaginations. But I think it is most important that we *should* be able to do so. A patient who has no dreams is also likely to have no imagination; that becomes a significant symptom, a sign which we should recognize.

Repeating this slightly differently and referring again to the group: Victor Hugo says, in "Les Légends des Siècles", that the emotion shared by two opposing armies in war is terror. If you are a member of one army you know that you are terrified; but you imagine that the enemy are all brave and disciplined fighters. In World War I there occurred one Christmas Day a fraternization between the opposed armies. The reason why the troops could fraternize was that they all knew what it was like to be at war. The Staff were somewhat withdrawn from the actual combatant experience, so they could see that, from a military point of view, to emerge from your trenches and greet the enemy was to give them important information about your numbers and your position. So the Command—on both sides— forbade any further fraternization at all. That experience never occurred again — either in the first World War or in the second; chivalry was killed.

In the shared emotional experience of the analysis the analyst is somewhat in the position of the officer who is obliged to think clearly. It sounds so simple — especially if you have never had an analysis.

I want to turn now to what we, as analysts, should observe in the analytic experience. What are the facts which we are supposed to observe? How do they come to us?

To consider this matter in an academic fashion — in the way in which we can when we are not practising analysis, but are discussing it here — I want to suggest that we do not in fact see or observe what we ordinarily think of as 'facts'. At first the analyst is ignorant of what is happening; if we are honest we have to admit that we haven't the faintest idea of what is going on. But if we stay, if we don't run away, if we go on observing the patient, after a time "a pattern will emerge".* That is possible when we are concerned with physically sensible facts — in short, all that our senses bring to us. The problem then is, what is our interpretation of the facts which our senses are making available to us? In other words, there has to be what we call an 'interpretation' of what our senses tell us.

There is a great deal of what I would call 'evidence' which makes me think that there is such a thing as a mind. Suppose this word 'mind' is not referring to a figment of the imagination, but to a peculiar kind of 'fact'. Cats and dogs appear to behave as if they have minds; I see no reason for supposing that there is any fundamental change when one of these animals learns the trick of walking on its two back legs, and later calls itself 'Homo Sapiens'. How does that fact — if it is a fact — come over to us who are observing the person? In addition to the evidence which our senses give us there is the evidence which is brought to us not by our sight, but by our *insight*. That is another 'fiction'. So I want to introduce — borrowing from Kant — the idea of *rational conjecture*. I want also to add to that *imaginative conjecture*. When we are waiting for this pattern to emerge we should also be sensitive to our imaginative conjectures and our rational conjectures as a part of the pattern which will perhaps become clearer to a point where we could translate it into words which we would try to communicate to the patient.

Q. My question is in the form of a fable. A scientist had a little fish in an aquarium. One day the little fish jumped out of the aquarium and the scientist observed that it could survive for five minutes. The next day the little fish repeated the feat and was able to survive for ten minutes. A day came when the fish was able to survive outside the water altogether and accompanied the scientist to the cinema, the theatre, everywhere. One day there was a storm and when the scientist went outside into the street with the fish, it fell into a little puddle and drowned. The moral of this fable is: Learning new things, but forgetting what has been learned before, is highly dangerous. Using this model, what would be the implications, in the patient/analyst relationship, if the analyst, while delving into unknown situations, the 'unknowable', gets catastrophically lost and destroys a therapeutic situation?

B. When the patient comes to the consulting room which animal has come? The scientist? Or one of these little creatures we have just

*Freud quoting from Charcot

been hearing about? And to which are you going to talk? Most patients were familiar with a Kleinian experience when they were infants; but they couldn't tell anybody what that experience was because they had not learnt the language necessary to make inter-pretations, diagnoses, verbal communications. After many years they acquire a considerable vocabulary but by that time they have forgotten what they wanted to say,* so they are as far off from communicating with somebody else as they were when they were full-term fetuses or amphibians, or even leading fishy existences surrounded with amniotic fluid.

There are two people in the consulting room, both of whom are in a peculiar state of mind—the state of mind in which we are when we are awake with our senses about us. That state of mind is different from the one in which we are when we are asleep. We are also in a different state of mind when we move about in a gaseous fluid from that in which we are when we exist in a watery medium. I expect you have all seen a new-born baby who can be put on a pot and its bottom seems to know what it is supposed to do. But I am told by psychiatrists that it cannot because its fibres are not myelinated. So I observe an impossible fact; that is the trouble with facts – they are all impossible. If you wrote the true story of your life between the time when you were born and the time now when you are here in this room, and if you were to say there were a lot of other people making a similar journey and that they came together in this room in São Paulo on April 3, 1978, nobody would believe it — everybody would know it was so impossible that it wouldn't be worth reading such rubbish. Similarly with the baby and its non-myelinated fibres—who or what told it what to do when it felt a pot under its bottom? Of course, the baby — to indulge in some more imagination— might decide that it wanted to keep its products to itself, and the individual with its fibres all myelinated would be upset because the baby was constipated. So how would you deal with this situation involving the well-trained, myelinated, scientific grown-up, and the non-myelinated, unscientific little animal which has just turned up?

I think we ought to consider whether what I have been talking about is worth discussing. What difference does it make if the patient had these pre-natal experiences? What does it matter if the patient has come as a grown, mature human being into the office and shows signs which we might be inclined to believe are terror and dread of a kind that could be described as 'sub-thalamic' fear?— in terms of the Grid, beta- and alpha-elements, physical facts. Is it any business of ours as psycho-analysts? Is there any point in being

*Melanie Klein did not forget. She was able to say it, but by then what she said comes to us as unfamiliar and peculiar.

sensitive to facts which are indistinguishable from imaginative conjectures? If the patient is able to have anxiety which he expresses by saying, "Doctor, I am afraid I am going mad", and we think that something is breaking in, interfering and interrupting his process of ordinary articulate verbal thinking, can we say anything to that same articulate individual which would seep back through the same route by which it floated up, and express itself in articulate and apparently rational ideas?

Referring to the fable we have just heard: Which animal should we talk to? And what language do we talk? What language do you talk if your dog chases a cat up a tree? Do you talk Portuguese? Or French? Or English? And why do you think that animal understands? Why do you think the animal will stop chasing the cat up the tree? Could we talk to this patient in some language which would be understood at the address to which we would want it to go? If this is something primitive such as in a state of panic fear — remembering again the god Pan, and the adrenals, and the autonomic and sympathetic telephonic communications — what language do we talk which would be understood by the adrenals and make them stop running away from the enemy or madly against him?

There are certain areas such as the caudate nucleus, the optic chiasmas, where the wires seem to cross. So perhaps if we can talk to the area which has the cerebral hemispheres at its disposal and information made available by the sympathetic and parasympathetic fibres, the communication could travel in both directions – to the 'cerebral spheres' and to the 'origin'.

TWO

B. I continue where we left off, considering the problem of giving the patient an interpretation which is addressed to a particular aspect of his statement. We listen to the statement, but we also observe what we consider to be the personality. I don't know how we could satisfy a scientist who asked, "What is a personality?" It is not very satisfactory to look up the word in a dictionary.

I recall a patient who talked freely and easily; he said that he didn't have dreams and that he had no imagination. For month after month he came to every session, never failed, never had an illness, never caught cold. When he got onto the couch he seemed to have some difficulty about which I did not bother much because it appeared to be simply a question of adjusting his clothes and his comfort. But after about three months I began to think this was very peculiar. He always lay in a slightly awkward position on the couch; he would lie flat and then raise his head as if he were struggling against some sort of opposition and trying to see his feet. He did that three or four times. I had no idea what he was doing or even how to tell myself what this peculiar movement was. He was so co-operative, so rational, and I was kept very well informed. He said that he only slept an hour or two each night and worked for about sixteen hours a day, seven days a week. There were no complaints when I took a break or at week-ends; no disturbance, no depression, whereas with other patients I am used to some kind of reaction to the fact that I am stopping.

I thought I would change my vertex because I could not see anything very much from where I was observing the patient. When I did that, it occurred to me that his precise and exact position on the couch could be comprehensible if he were lying on the edge of a precipice. And then his posture began to look like a cataleptic attitude. Indeed, the whole analysis began to look like a compulsive ritual— the same hour, the same behaviour, no diversion from that position at all. The more I saw of him the more I thought that these were not ordinary communications and that my interpretations themselves fitted into the pattern. I wondered what kind of psychiatric diagnosis I could make. The nearest I could get to one was that the total situation in the consulting room was a folie à deux, and that I was just playing a part in this relationship. Then I began to look at and listen to the behaviour of both these people, one of whom was myself. I continued to observe and listen to that peculiar conversation. The 'free associations' and the interpretations fitted in beautifully. You could call it the marriage of two minds — but there was something wrong with it. You could not call it homosexual; you could not call it heterosexual. In fact you could not call it sexual at all — not if the word 'sex' means the kind of thing that it means in botany, or physiology, or what I call psycho-analysis.

I managed to effect some change, because as the pattern became clear to me I felt I could also make it clear to the patient. I found a number of formulations which made it comprehensible to the patient that I had parted from him. Then it appeared that this same relationship existed between him and somebody else. I interpreted that the deficiency had been made good by his being able to enlist the co-operation of some other member of the public with which he had social relationships. After some time a change occurred again; now

he fell back into having the same sort of relationship with himself —
so I interpreted that. But I wondered what this 'Self' was. What does
it mean — him Self, her Self, my Self? I found it unsatisfactory to
talk about his 'body' and his 'mind' because both those words have a
large aura of meaning. The body is a thing that you take to your
physician; the mind you don't bother with. Indeed, if one talked
about his 'mind' it was like talking about some unsupportable
fiction, like talking about God to an aetheist. The patient listened to
the noise I was making, but it was devoid of content.

I tried giving it a location; I talked about his 'feelings', and the
sort of thing he did 'up here', in his head. It was clear that he did not
understand what I meant —or thought it was just nonsense anyway.
He didn't say that; he was polite —he simply ignored any reference
to 'up here' or 'down there'. So I fell back on still talking about his
'Self'. I said, "Now you are talking as if your Self was located in
your spleen". Sometimes I could have said that it was located in his
adrenals, but I didn't have to because he talked about people who
'ran away', or people who were 'very aggressive'. I was able to say,
"This person who you say runs away, and this person you say is very
aggressive, are the same person. I think they are your Self". This
peculiar mobility became more and more pronounced; I had to go on
chasing this Self around what seemed to be various anatomical areas.

It became evident that the Self was not within the limits of what I
call the body. I had to extend my interpretations over an area which
had different boundaries —indeed it had *no* boundaries. In order to
express it at all I would have to borrow a term like 'infinity'.
It reminded me of Milton's words which express it so well:
"Won from the void and formless infinite". He speaks about being
"long detained in that obscure sojourn"; about outer and inner darkness, middle darkness and "up to re-ascend though hard and rare".
That is a good description of this patient, as if he had descended into
what psycho-analysts call 'the unconscious' and remained there a
long time —"though long detained in that obscure sojourn", "and up
to re-ascend". But when he does re-ascend, instead of emerging into
the realms of light, he finds himself blinded.

Melanie Klein gave me an interpretation which puzzled me for a
long time. She said, "You feel mutilated, castrated, as you emerge
from the womb". That sounded like pure nonsense to me. By that
time I was also seeing a patient, so I thought I would try it out on him
too. Between us there seemed to be some truth in it; it did seem as if
getting born was a dangerous experience in which the mother, or the
mother's genitalia mutilated the baby. Further experience over the
years had made me feel that this is also true in the many re-births
which could be said to take place between the time when we are

born — in the obstetrical sense — and the time when we die. This includes the time when we emerge from one state of mind into another.

What about waking up? The state of mind in which we are now is one in which we have our senses— in the neurological sense—active. But we do not know what we do, and what we see, and where we go when we are in the state of mind in which we are when we are asleep. People talk readily about having "had a dream last night"; it is difficult to point out to them that one would like to ask, "How did you know it was a dream?" The patient I have been talking about was quite right—he didn't dream. When, according to most of us, he was in bed and asleep he went to places and he saw things just as much as he did when he was awake. But dream? No. That is the sort of thing that is done by people who have dreams, who go to bed and go to sleep; but not to people like my patient. People like that don't get ill; they don't have dreams. However, such a person is also extremely intelligent; so he learns the kind of language that I talk and says, "I had a dream last night", and then tells me a story which I think sounds like a perfectly ordinary fact. When he said he had a dream, met so-and-so and was very annoyed with him, he had in fact done so. I knew because I heard the story from that same person of whom he had 'dreamed' who also came to me for analysis.

What language ought I to have talked to this patient? And what should I have said to him if I knew that language? It is clear that the language he was talking was extremely accurate; I could rely on his statements as easily as I could rely on his coming to the consulting room with such accuracy that I could correct my watch by the time of his arrival. There was no question of his being late — my watch might be fast or slow, but not he. I don't know what clock he was going by, but he was right. So in fact I cannot tell you anything about how to analyse that patient, but I hope you will be able to tell me something.

Q. What is the relationship between memory and intuition on the one hand, and your concept of thoughts without a thinker on the other?

B. To take the last point first: Let us imagine that when a number of people collect together like this, there are stray thoughts floating around trying to find a mind to settle in. Can we as individuals catch one of these wild thoughts without being too particular about what race or category it is, whether it is a memory or an intuition, and however strange or however savage or friendly it might be, give it a home and then allow it to escape from your mouth — in other words, give it birth. To put it in other terms, can we catch a germ of an idea and plant it where it can begin to develop until it is mature enough for it to be born? We do not have immediately to expel the wild thought or the germ of an idea until we think it would be viable if it were made public. When we make it public, then we can have a look at it and decide whether to call it a memory, or an intuition, or a prediction, a prophetic statement, or even a diseased germ.*

If you were analysing a child you could say, "I see you have brought your baby" — it might be a doll or a piece of cloth. If the child says, "I haven't got a baby; I couldn't have a baby", then you might say, "Perhaps it hasn't been born yet". That would be the germ of an idea, or the germ of an unborn child, the child that hasn't happened yet.

Parents say, "Why can't you children play properly? what are you quarrelling and fighting about all the time?" But the children don't know what they are fighting about; they would have to be prophets to know. Similarly with the thought without a thinker, the thought which is looking for somebody in whom 'it could be thought about'; or, from the point of view of us as individuals, the wild thought which is in the air but which nobody has dared to think so far because we are afraid of being asked, "Why are you playing with that dirty idea? Why do you play with these nasty thoughts? You ought to be good — a nice girl, a nice boy, a nice psycho-analyst". It is difficult to stick to one's right to be a nasty psycho-analyst who has nasty thoughts and who is willing to give a home to still more nasty thoughts. I suggest that you do that with one of these wild thoughts whether it be called dirty, nasty, psychotic, banal or ordinary. There is no shortage of abusive terms for the idea. You might even, in spite of everything, call it 'Narcissus'. It could admire itself in a mirror or pool of water. But "Fluctuat nec murgitur" — don't let the nice little Narcissus fall into the pool in which it is admiring its features, and get drowned. When you have one of these wild thoughts, or one of these germs of a wild idea, you need to have the courage to protect it from people who want to dispose of it or send it to a psychiatric hospital — for the best of reasons, of course. It is much better to shut up Solzhenitsyn where he would be properly looked after and cared for instead of running about wild. So, whether your child is called Narcissus or whether it is called Solzhenitsyn, you need to be able to look after it — or somebody else will look after it for you.

Has anybody else any wild thoughts?

Q. Using your illustration of the two fighting armies (who do not reveal anything known and therefore keep up the tension of the

*It would be easier to detect and to think about the germ of a disease. I think the analyst has to exercise discrimination with regard to ideas that come to his mind.

unknown) as a model of the psycho-analytic work, to what extent can psycho-analysis cause the 'disease', just as soldiers may become mad in war?

B. There is always a chance that the opposed armies, on the strength of the shared emotion of terror, will fraternize. As for the individual, I remember one of my men, a young fellow of about nineteen, who began to smile in an extremely irritating manner. The senior N.C.O. wanted to have him punished for a crime which was called 'dumb insolence'. That smile was peculiarly irritating in the sense that neurologists talk about the nerve which is irritated and also in the sense in which socially we talk about being annoyed. The question was, who had gone mad? Who was in-sane? Un-healthy? We, who kept on fighting? Or this boy who had had a psychotic breakdown? Was it a burst of common sense which had broken out in him, while the rest of us when on with our shared psychosis, our continuous, murderous marriage with the enemy? Lots of people were frightened of breaking out; in the airforce crews were afraid that they only had to go on flying combatant missions long enough and they would get killed. It is dangerous enough flying around anyway; it is insane to fly about when people are firing guns at you. What were these fighting pilots afraid of? Becoming ill? Or becoming sane? So far we seem capable of having a mass psychosis in which we all agree to go about in disciplined and organized gangs of murderers, dedicated to the destruction of people who wear different clothes. Sometimes we don't even bother with the uniform if we can say, "I am black; he is white; therefore he is wrong". Or, "I am white and he is black and therefore he is wrong". The colour of the skin saves us the trouble of going inside that skin. And yet *we* are addicted to respecting the individual; we treat individuals as if they mattered. And in many ways we behave as if it is a good thing to help an individual to be one who has thoughts and ideas of his own. Unfortunately our dedication to that ideal seems to be slender; while we are dedicated to the rights of an individual to have thoughts or ideas of his own, before we know what has happened we have become 'Kleinians' or —

I*—I would like to know what 'Kleinian' means—

B. You are optimistic. Even Mrs. Klein didn't know what it meant— she protested at being called a 'Kleinian'. But, as Betty Joseph told her, "You are too late—you are Kleinian whether you like it or not". There was nothing she could do about it. So— although we aspire to respect the individual, bigotry rears its ugly head again. While

*Interpreter

I have the aspiration to respect individuals it does not suprise me at all to find that I am bigoted about something else.

Q. Why do certain patients try to keep things the way they are — they don't want to get cured, have no faith in getting better, prefer illness. What is it that makes them avoid getting better?

B. It depends who says it is "better". As I have said before, when a quadruped got onto its hind legs and walked on two feet instead of four it started trouble. Not only does it have to be a very capable athlete to be able to balance on two feet instead of four; imagine the difficulty when our nervous system developed cerebral spheres, when our body, which was a happy dinosaur, suddenly started turning into a mammal and then the poor mammal started growing a mind. That is where we are now. We seem to have minds; then our minds have brain children which are a nuisance. So it is not surprising that we hate thinking and anything that makes us think.

It is clear that we should think properly, but where do we do our thinking? Up in our heads? Or down on our two feet that have to walk around? Or in our genitalia? Or our diaphragm? Or some part of our hypochondria? We don't like hypochondriacs; but suppose we have to do our thinking with the co-operation of our hypo-chondria. Sometimes it seems as if we have to do our thinking with something which is very thin, like a diaphragm. Being balanced on the knife edge of a diaphragm is even more difficult than lying on the thin edge of a precipice — or even a couch. You are liable to fall onto the floor — or to fall on the other side and be quite comfortable. Some people prefer the knife edge — they are frightened of being well off, they are frightened of being comfortable. We might say, "And down to descend to that obscure sojourn and be long detained there in middle and outer darkness".

This is the problem: Thinking is a development which is very unwelcome; unwelcome because it might make us more comfortable; unwelcome because it might make us more uncomfortable. It is difficult to know what to do with the capacity to think.

THREE

B. Before I start airing some more views perhaps you would like to raise any topics which you think need to have further exploration.

Q. How can an observer say that another person is thinking thoughts or not thinking thoughts?

Q. You described how you changed your vertex the better to understand what was happening with a patient. I would like you to talk more about this.

Q. The object of life is to get closer to the truth. How far would you consider madness the only way to get closer to reality?

Q. I would like you to say more about rational conjectures and imaginative conjectures.

Q. I would like you to speak about the specific communication within an analysis. Also, the difference between psycho-analytic conversation and other kinds of talk.

B. First, I will try to approach this profound question of getting to know the truth. To take a simple example: An infant sees something that it wants and discovers that it is out of reach. So it starts to crawl towards it. In this way it is reacting in a complex fashion. It is difficult to say of what it is thinking because the infant may not have learnt how to use its own methods of communication. As far as crawling to the object is concerned it discovers that it is very hard work. I don't know how it learns to use its 'voluntary musculature' as we call it; it is already a complex activity. It involves the use of the eyes; it involves the activation of an ambition to reach whatever it is that is out of reach. To answer the question — How do we know the infant is thinking thoughts? — we have to resort to imaginative conjecture. We cannot ask the child, and there is no way of thinking about what it is thinking about. But if the baby starts crawling towards the fire because the flames look so pretty, then the imaginative conjecture can become a rational conjecture — you still don't know what it is trying to do, but you can think it may be going to take hold of a pretty piece of fire. So the observer, the mother, father or nurse, begins to feel a certain degree of alarm and gets ready to stop the child from putting its hand on the coals of fire. As the child makes further elements of an approach towards the fire the observer translates his rational conjectures into something like probabilities and prepares to make muscular movements to get between the baby and the fire. In the meantime the baby may have become tired, cannot be supported by its four limbs and bumps its head. So the ground hurts it. I don't know how it is done, but the baby resorts to its vocal chords and lets out a yell. What is the interpretation of that yell? It seems to be as undifferentiated as, say, a motor horn. When you are walking, or driving in a car, you have to translate that motor horn; you have to decide what the address is to which it is being directed and then make up your mind whether you will do anything about it or not. Getting back to the baby, I don't think the mother would have to go through a long and obscure series of thoughts; if she were capable of being concerned for the child she would pick it up and soothe it because it was hurt. It will be a black day for babies if mothers have to have a psycho-analysis before they can pick up their babies and kiss them. Perhaps we shall come to that one of these days, but in the meantime I hope we shall be wild and natural enough to go straight to the point.

A lot can happen between the time when the baby is learning to crawl and the time when the baby is driving a motor car and listening to, or interpreting, or sounding its horn. This raises another series of questions: How old is the baby when it learns to cry? How old is the grown-up who is driving the car? It is an important question because the ability to drive a car is a technical accomplishment; it is more easily achieved and can develop faster than its wisdom. Conversely, a baby could be wiser than a grown-up, especially a grown-up who is so technically equipped that he would have to go through all these analytic processes before deciding to intervene between the baby and the fire. But are the tests adequate to answer the problem of whether a person is wise enough to be allowed to drive a car? Tragic accidents occur because a child is athletically able to ride a bicycle; it can do so as soon as it gets a chance of escaping from parental prohibitions. But the child hasn't enough wisdom to know that that little bicycle ride may change its life completely, either because it gets knocked down and badly injured, or, more tragically, it is killed. How is the parent to make available to the child that degree of wisdom he or she has acquired?

Q. This is a story, used as an analogy, of an expedition to the Amazon jungle in which a group of people got lost. One of them was so frightened that he shot a mortar into some trees. Consequently enormous pieces of wood came clattering down and killed some of the group. Nevertheless this accident also opened up a hole in the dense vegetation so that it was possible to use it to send up a smoke signal for help. The analogy I want to make is with the opening up of new ways through a careless act of destruction; and with the risk of using thinking to propagate non-thinking.

B. Nowadays not only the vegetable world but the animal world also is getting too crowded. To clear a space we could employ a very effective but somewhat indiscriminate method of clearance, one not much more discriminating than the baby's yell or the motorist's horn, but much more powerful — an atomic bomb; or a 'new and improved' atomic bomb, a neutron bomb. That would clear quite a space for other forms of life. In this way the human animal is now able to get rid of itself and make room for some improved form of life, maybe something which is impervious to what to us are lethal rays.

[There followed a discussion about the Portuguese translation of 'impervious' — Ed.]

B. Somebody has let loose a verbal bomb! So far it has only started us thinking which we hope is less lethal than the neutron bomb. So possibly the intervention of the delaying action of thought between the impulse and its immediate action may produce enough time for second thoughts. Otherwise first thoughts will be enough.

In the Apocrypha — Ecclesiasticus — there is a saying, "Wisdom cometh to the learned man through opportunity for leisure". But the person has to be learned first and then has to have leisure enough to enable him to become wise. The problem is that learned men can produce and perfect a neutron bomb possibly faster than we can provide the leisure to think. It is so often a matter of acting first and repenting at leisure.

Q. I would like to suggest a model. A geologist went out with his dog in search of rocks. He tried to rid himself of the memory of past things in order to grasp new knowledge. But he lost his way and became very hungry. He finally killed his dog and ate it. Afterwards, seeing the scattered bones on the ground, he started to lament, "What a pity my dog isn't here to eat all these bones." The moral is one of St. Augustine's sayings; "In order to cultivate the spirit and reason it is necessary first of all to cultivate one's bodily needs". This model refers to events that occur between a patient and his analyst; what is this catastrophic situation between the geologist and his dog in their expedition to explore the unknown?

B. St. Augustine had good reason to know that the great Roman Empire had gone. The only things that were left were the bones of the martyrs. He proposed in the place of the destroyed Roman Empire to erect the City of God. Today we can have an idea of what point in this story we have reached. We can hear this imaginative conjecture — the fable — and compare it with where we have got to in that story. The fable could be said to have turned into history, and the history is a pageant in which we are now ourselves taking part.

I would like now to say more in answer to the question about the vertex. I borrow the word from mathematics, but there is a difficulty about borrowing these words to use them for a different purpose from that for which they were created. I do so not because I want to make things more difficult, but because the existing meaning of the word tends to create a difficulty when it is being used in a new way and in a new context. There is nothing new about that difficulty. For example, Euclid elaborated geometry. It was useful and has lasted for over two thousand years. But Euclidean geometry runs into difficulties when it comes to the question of parallel lines. If you could walk between those two lines you might gradually come to the end, and by that time they would be wide apart. If you turned round and looked back to where you had come from you would find that the parallel lines had come together behind you. This is similar to what happens if you live long enough; the problems which have been solved become unsolved because you have changed; therefore all the relationships that you had have changed. The relationship between you and your home is different at the age of one from that at the age of two or three. I am not talking about A or B, but the *relationship between* A and B, the part in between, the umbilical chord, whatever takes the place of the umbilical chord, whatever it is that connects you with your parents and your parents' parents, and with all the other objects with which you have a relationship. If Euclid could return today he might want to know what algebraic projective geometry is. He would have difficulty with it because there would be no lines or circles or other pictorial images. But can one say that algebraic geometry is superior to Euclidean geometry? There is no real conflict; algebraic geometry was *implicit* in Euclidean geometry, and what was implicit has now been made *explicit*. So Euclid might in time begin to recognize his brain children.

It might be helpful if we were sufficiently flexible to change our vertex so that we could look at ourselves. Cortez, according to Keats,* could stand "silent upon a peak in Darien" with "a wild surmise", a wild thought, an imaginative conjecture, and see the world that he had discovered and what it looks like today— that is assuming that Cortez was sufficiently flexible. Can we do anything to keep our mental muscles in good working? For this purpose it would be useful to have a grid which we could mentally climb around. If we could turn the Grid then the distances between the lines

*On First Looking into Chapman's Homer

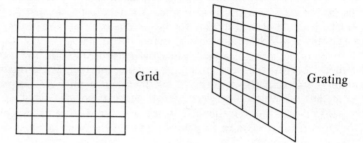

Grid   Grating

would become very fine — the Grid can be turned into a Grating.

Putting it in another way: Newton's description of optics can be considered in terms of wave lengths; the distance between the climax of one wave and the next is quite large. But by changing your vertex you can make it much smaller; you can measure the distance between ultra-violet and infra-red with some very fine gradations, in terms of angstrom units.

We use certain words, like 'love' and 'hate', in a crude way; each can be split into intermediate gradations. For example, the baby might love bright colours and food that tasted nice. Still in the 'love' category as it were, adult love can become passionate love, and the passionate love can become 'spiritual' love. As analysts we can see all this in any relationship between the patient's Self and our Self. What about this bit in between? What about what we call an 'analogy'? In the analogy the two anchors don't matter very much, but the bit in between does matter. I think that is what Freud is driving at when he talks about the 'transference'; he means the bit in between the patient's Self and the analyst's Self.

The transference is transient, it is temporary; it is not the same at the end of a session as it is at the beginning. The beginning and the end of the session is a crude division. We need to be able to look at it through a Grating in which the divisions are not fifty-five minutes or ten minutes or ten seconds. When it is a question of drawing attention to the relationship between the analyst and the analysand we have to judge the *speed* of the change because some patients have a lot of difficulty in judging time and distance. A patient may come ten mintues late, wants to leave five mintues early, looks at his watch and says, "I must go — that was a very short session!" He is surprised; he doesn't know what has happened to that session — why is it so short? Or the patient doesn't bother about thinking which slows up things so much between the impulse and the action, has the impulse to leave and goes without thinking; it is much quicker. I have had the experience in which I was in Los Angeles and the patient wanted to come and see me, but he found he was in London because he went from Los Angeles to London without wasting time in thinking first — went straight from the impulse to the action.

We are concerned with having respect for thinking, how to think clearly and how to pass it on. We not only have to learn to think in such a way that we understand what we are thinking about, but we have to translate it into some form which our analysands or others will be able to understand. This is something that artists seem to be able to do; if we read of Shakespeare's case histories which we call a 'play' it still reminds us of real people. How many psycho-analytical papers remind of real people? Beethoven could write marks on a piece of paper which some people can translate into musical sounds that make us feel we know what he meant. Leonardo could 'draw a line round' what he saw so that *we* can still see what he thought a human being looked like; Giotto let us see what he thought God looked like. What form of artists can we be, and what work of art can we produce so that some of our offspring will be able to understand what we want to transmit?

FOUR

B. We who occupy a certain position in the story of the development of the human culture can know a little about the history of where we have come from so far and, if we look back on our road, the route we have followed. But it is difficult to know what words to use when we want to talk about the 'road' or the 'route' which psycho-analysts are trying to follow. There are so many histories — of religion, mathematics, economics, civilization — but how would you write the history of psycho-analysis? Where would you start it? Which is the origin from which it springs? How have we got from there to here? It is hard to see — to fall back on a sort of psycho-analytically oriented genealogical history — who are our ancestors and what way our offspring are going. If we talk about genetic history we could suppose that the process followed Mendelian laws: A distinction was made between what were supposed to be the laws of inheritance, which followed Mendelian laws, and other things which were considered to be acquired characteristics, transmissible. But

Mendelian laws don't help us much in considering the question of the inheritance of psycho-analytic development. It is convenient to talk about the "British Psycho-analytic Society", the "French Psycho-analytic Society", the "Brazilian", and so on; at first sight it would appear that that probably followed Mendelian laws. But when we think that we are discussing the mind or the personality or the character, then it becomes difficult to say what laws that inheritance follows. We could say: Who has inherited Freud's ideas? Obviously Mendelian inheritance would be useful — Freud's children and Freud's grandchildren. But suppose we think that people who had no blood relationship with Freud had something to do with this story; how do they come to have psycho-analytic ideas? Who or what are these people, and where do they come in the story?

Last time I mentioned that Euclid might not be able to recognize the statements and formulations of algebraic projective geometry. If Freud came back today would he understand what we are talking about? Would he recognize what we say is psycho-analysis? Or would he say, "These aren't my children; these are bastards"? He might have to readjust his views about his progeny — all these theories and ideas which have sprouted up. In fact, the trouble started when Freud was still alive. He and Jung and Stekel got together and admitted that Freud was the only one who was entitled to consider that what he had said was psycho-analysis *was* psycho-analysis. It was agreed that Jung would call his school 'analytical psychology', and Stekel would call his 'individual psychology'. So they were split up; what had started as one became three. Now each of the three has split up into many more — poly-psychological. So we could say that we have lost track of the psycho-analytic line of inheritance. Yet we feel that we would like to say, "This is the Way; this is the Way from which we must not diverge too much. We should remain free to have our own ideas and opinions, but not too far from the Way."

The Way played a big part in the history of human civilization long before anybody had heard or thought of what Freud called psycho-analysis. A Chinese monk* wrote about The Tao, The Way. Biologists think we have diverted, that we are a branch of the Simian inheritance. So even by making mistakes we are sometimes right.

I wonder if it is within the rules of psycho-analysis to be·able to laugh at ourselves? Is it according to the rules of psycho-analysis that we should be amused and find things funny? Is it permissible to enjoy a psycho-analytic meeting? I suggest that, having broken through in this revolutionary matter of being amused in the sacred

* [Translated in error as 'monkey' – Ed.]

progress of psycho-analysis, we might as well continue to see where that more joyous state of mind might take us.

Q. These discussions have usually focussed or the catastrophic aspects of destructiveness. I would like to suggest another side — something lighter and happier. I submit some clinical material which I gathered during supervision of a case with an eight year old boy.

He begins a session by making a plasticine ball and then suggests a game of football between a boy and a girl. He soon leaves this game and picks up a box of coloured pencils, empties it and brings it up to his eyes, giving the impression that he is looking at his analyst through binoculars. The analyst says that when he uses the box in that way he is able to see her even when she is far away, for example, when he looks at her at the club on Sundays. The boy asks her what time it is and puts the box on the table saying that it is a tunnel. He puts his hand through it and, picking up the plasticine ball and a doll, he adds, "this is a machine that changes things. When I put a doll inside it a girl comes out". The analyst says, "It is like a mother into whom a father goes and a baby comes out". After hearing this interpretation the boy continues to play more enthusiastically with his 'tunnel of transformation' saying, "A cup goes in, a doll comes out; a doll goes in, a cup comes out". The analyst then repeats the interpretation she gave him before.

I want to call attention to this 'tunnel of transformation' that this child uses with such enthusiasm and happiness during a session, discovering something new without the need of destructiveness.

I have noticed that we refer to a fear of the disappearance of psycho-analysis. Does this fear lead us into a protective attitude towards psycho-analysis? Or does it cause us to leave psycho-analysis unprotected by an over-protectiveness, contributing unknowingly to its disappearance by suffocating it?

B. That is a striking example. I wonder if others are as impressed as I am, before I take up the train of thought it arouses in me.

O. In Rio de Janeiro there are two Psycho-analytical Societies and two Group Societies. Analysts belonging to the Psycho-analytical Society usually also belong to the Group Society; the same people belonging to one society belong to the other. So that the problems that befall the Psycho-analytical Society are basically the same as those of the Group Society. For example, in both societies the subject concerning the admittance of non-medical students is discussed. The degree of passionate involvement in these discussions reaches an almost violent level when the discussion takes place in a psycho-analytic society meeting. When this same problem is discussed in the

Group Society with the same people present, the same level of destructiveness is not reached. I repeat; the members are the same in one society as they are in the other.

B. One of the advantages of a group of people — for example, this meeting itself — is that you can often see something spread out amongst all of us which in the individual psycho-analysis one sees in a more precise way. Freud himself seemed to be disconcerted when the first International Congress was held; he thought they could all get together. Instead of that it appeared that they all fell out with each other. So instead of leading to a union of views, it led to a great diversity of views.

The story of the Tower of Babel crops up again and again. It seems that when people unite to storm the citadel of the human mind they fall apart in a primitive way; they join in order to run away from something or to fight something. That seems to me to be a spread-out example, as if the body politic were developing a kind of adrenal activity. In a physical human body one could say that the human embryo was beginning to bud off the adrenals which sooner or later would begin to produce adrenalin. But so does the human group; whatever scientific products they produce, they also seem to produce a great deal of adrenalin. So you can detect a primitive, emotional reaction. The individual human being, according to genetic theory, seems to be produced by the fusion of gametes which are derived both from the man and the woman. But since the individual has a father *and* a mother it is not surprising that it has characteristics which are both male and female.

Rio, I gather, has two societies; that when the people get together in one of them they behave in a somewhat masculine or aggressive manner; when the same people get together in another society they behave in a passive manner. Are there male and female societies? They are composed of the same people, so it it no good asking the obstetricians. I think we would have to ask psycho-analysts — in fact, ourselves.

Now I want to draw attention to something which I constantly come across — psycho-analytic pessimism. Milton, when he was not yet twenty years old, protested against what he called being "sunk in an Oedipean gloom". I sometimes think that analysts are sunk in this same Oedipean gloom; so much so that they are often taken by surprise when they discover that there is such a thing as mental pain. One feels that they have only learnt that there is a *theory* that there is mental pain but that they don't believe it exists, or that psycho-analysis is a method of treating it. So when a patient gets 'better' they are surprised; they don't believe it has anything to do with the work they are doing. The clinical example about the child is important because it is a reminder that patients do become happier and more able to be creative or constructive, and change from being primitively dominated by flight and fighting. After all, embryos develop; they don't only have adrenal glands. Other portions of the anatomy develop in the embryo itself, and life, with any luck, does not stop short at birth. The full-term fetus continues to grow after birth, so although it may start by running away from or fighting its brother or sister it also begins to grow out of that stage. The psychoanalytic procedure does a great deal to help that development to take place, just as much as the work of pediatricians helps to keep babies and children healthy so that they can go on developing. Psycho-analysis helps the spirit, or soul, or super-soul, or ego, or id, or super-ego — whatever name you want to give it — to continue. Plato describes in the Theatitus how Socrates says that he is a kind of mental midwife. I don't see why we should not claim mental development, mental ancestors, one of them being Socrates himself. If that is so, we too could say we are a modern version of mental midwives; we help the soul or psyche to be born, and even help it to continue to develop *after* it is born. We should not consider ourselves to be simply historians of the past grandeurs of psychoanalysis. We are not dead yet and there is no necessity to spend our time attending our own funeral service. I don't find it interesting to be perpetually celebrating the obsequies of psycho-analysis; I like also to be attending one of its many re-births.

While we do not want to forget our famous men let us by all means praise famous men and women of our own time, our mothers as well as our fathers, because even our mothers had something to do with begetting us, so they might as well be given a passing reference sometimes. I hope that the masculine society in Rio will occasionally say "How do you do?" to the more passive society — even if they are the same people.

0. I would like to present for your consideration the observations made by the physicist, Werner Heisenberg, and by a psycho-analyst, Luis Chiozza.

Heisenberg asserted that it is impossible to calculate the trajectory of an electron because there is no such trajectory and that in the description of these phenomena it is impossible to separate the observer from the rest of nature, impossible to make a scientific observation when the interaction between observer and observed is ignored. This he called The Uncertainty Principle.

Luis Chiozza, an Argentinian training analyst, basing himself on Freud's writings about the sexual theory, "Instincts and their Vicissitudes", concludes that every psychical process constitutes a somatic matrix for qualitatively differentiated impulses. At the same time these impulses are unconscious, particular fantasies which he calls "specific fantasy".

Curious contributions to human thought! On the one hand we have a physicist — who deals with objective, rational and precise mechanisms — describing an Uncertainty Principle; on the other hand a psycho-analyst — who deals with subjective, irrational and imprecise resources—describing the Specific Fantasy.

B. A lot of people attach importance to what we call the 'truth'. Some of them are painters; some musicians; others mathematicians; some are psycho-analysts. I don't know what Freud meant by 'scientific method', but it seems to me that the basic idea is to bring truth to bear. I am not surprised that we think that some people are important painters; there is something about their work which makes us feel that they are not trying to make fools of us all; they are trying to show us the truth. The same is true of some sculptors who make structures which trap the light, sometimes with a piece of projecting material, sometimes with a hole which goes right through. If we look at the light which has been trapped then we may be able to see the truth which the sculptor is trying to show us. Mathematicians formulate projective algebraic formulae; they are not trying to make life more difficult; they are talking the simplest, most precise language they know. If we take the trouble to listen to what they are saying then we might learn something.

Psycho-analysts think that what we are trying to observe is disturbed by who we are. Judges in the law courts, trying to find out who is guilty, have also discovered that there are difficulties about answering the simple question — guilty or not guilty? Heisenberg has stated clearly his Uncertainty Principle, but in his search for the truth he discovered not only the Uncertainty Principle but the possibility that there is such a thing as uncertainty. But uncertainty has no colour, no smell; it is not palpable, but it exists. And in the course of this journey which the human race makes in its attempt to reach the truth we discover that we observers disturb the thing we are observing.

Even the most advanced human thinkers are only at an embryonic stage. We have only just started thinking; we do not even know the rules of thought; we do not know what to do with this newly acquired capacity for thinking. Heisenberg's Uncertainty Principle is an important stage in the journey; it is deplorable that any section of mankind should be *certain*. If there is anything which is certain it is that certainty is wrong.

FIVE

B. I have been explaining to the translator that I find it quite bac
enough trying to translate what I want to say into English; I am therefore very thankful that I don't have to try to translate it into any
other language. I would ask you to be indulgent to both of us. I don't
think it is our fault—it is inherent in the difficulty of the matter I want
to introduce. For that reason I think that this subject will probably
take at least four or five evenings to introduce. What I say will either
seem to be incomprehensible, or so obvious that it is hardly worth
saying. Whether it appears to be obscure or whether it appears to be
obvious, in either case it will give you a misleading impression.

I will start by reminding you of what Melanie Klein says about
projective identification and the depressive and paranoid
schizoid positions. The infant or very young child thinks it can split
off nasty feelings and ideas, that is, anything which is unpleasant.
According to her, the child has an *omnipotent phantasy* that it can
split off these unpleasant thoughts or ideas and then evacuate them
in the way that it can evacuate urine and faeces. She was referring
to something she believed to be applicable *after birth*.

What I am going to say cannot aspire to the status of what is
ordinarily called 'scientific thought'; the most that I can claim is that
it is imaginative conjecture. The central point of this guess is that
even before birth the fetus—I don't know how close to being a full-
term fetus, or whether it could apply to the embryo from an early
stage — becomes sensitive to what could be called 'happenings',
events like the sense of the pulsation of its blood, physical pressure
of a kind that can be communicated through a watery fluid such as
amniotic fluid or even extra-cellular fluid. (When I refer to extra-
cellular fluid I am talking about a fluid which is as near as
possible to something which is not polluted at all. The amniotic fluid
is already polluted by meconium.) I can conceive of situations in
which pressure is transmitted through the amniotic fluid and can
therefore possibly stimulate the optic and auditory pits. Here I am
guessing that even as embryo of three or four somites has something which will one day become what we call 'sensations'. I do not
know what they are to be called — if they exist at all — in the intra-
uterine period. Intra-uterine photography has shown the fetus with
its arm raised as if to protect itself against a bright light. I don't

know what that bright light would be unless it is the kind of light that one sees with changes of pressure on one's eyeball. The fetus can also be seen in these photographs sucking its thumb—indeed a child can actually be born with its thumb in its mouth. Both these bits of evidence seem to me to excuse rational conjectures. I certainly would not expect any scientific worker who is familiar with the discipline and the rigors of scientific thought to agree, but as psycho-analysts I think we have to fall back on such imaginative and rational conjectures. The whole of our subject could be attacked on the grounds that it is unscientific and cannot be supported by any scientific evidence. The most that could be claimed for it is that it is 'probable'.

I am supposing that the gametes of intelligent parents would be likely to fuse to produce what could be called an intelligent person I see no reason why a full-term fetus should not also be regarded as a potentially intelligent grown-up. All of this is what I call a rational conjecture: I don't think it is possible to claim any more for it than that, otherwise it is distorting, devaluating the standards of scientific work.

I can imagine that even the embryo could much dislike the feeling of blood pulsating through its system. Similarly, that it might dislike the effects of the early stages of production of adrenalin or other developing function. The more potentially sensitive or intelligent, the more it would be likely to be what could later be called 'aware of' these sensations, dislike them and therefore get rid of them. I think that what takes place at this stage is analogous to an omnipotent phantasy or scepticism; it is what will later be called a 'fact'. The fetus may take a wrong turning in development, become incapable of having 'feelings' or 'ideas' and so be born lacking important elements of its equipment. However, the post-natal creature still retains its potential for intelligent activity. Amongst these activities which are retained is a capacity for imitation, mimesis, so that the 'intelligent' (as distinct from 'wise') baby or child is able to imitate fathers, mothers, brothers, sisters,; it is 'well-adjusted'. Later, if the person is unfortunate enough to get into a court of law— as was the case with Loeb and Leopold—he could be judged according to what in England were known as the MacNaughton Rules: Does the accused know the difference between right and wrong? The kind of personality to which I am drawing attention—which could now be called by a psychiatrist a 'psychotic'— *does* know the difference between what is called right and wrong. Of course Loeb and Leopold knew that all these ordinary people call murder 'wrong'. So of course they knew that it was 'wrong' to commit what they called 'the perfect crime' and stuff the body of the murdered child into a drain — a scientific procedure which is not, by a sane person, called 'research'. So the barrister for the prosecution can justly argue that these people know the difference between right and wrong and are therefore guilty of the crime.

I mention this story to draw attention to the peculiar and frightening situation in which the very intelligent person is not capable of being wise. There are certain diseases in which there seems to be a defect in the domain of neuro-transmitters. For a long time there were difficulties because there was something anomalous about the research findings. Although the administration of Leva Dopa seemed to have a curative effect on Parkinsonism, it was recently discovered that what is apparently a *lack* of dopamine is not so at all — the total amount of dopamine remains unaltered. Therefore it is puzzling to know why there appears to be a shortage. It now looks possible that the truth lies in the abnormal concentration of dopamine *receptors* in certain parts of the nervous system. We analysts are faced with a similar paradox. Why is a person, who is apparently highly intelligent, lacking in wisdom? You would think such a person would naturally go on to be wise as well. Consider your own analytic experience. Have you ever come across people who you feel must be extremely intelligent in order to be so stupid. It sounds like a clever paradox to say, "There is no fool like a stupid fool; and there is no stupid fool like an intelligent one".* Why is it that so many highly intelligent people seem to be incapable of being wise? What has happened to the intelligence? Is it, like trees that hide the wood, too thick to perceive the wisdom that lies beyond the cleverness?

Q. What could you tell us about Freud's formulation that an analyst should go back to analysis every five years? Can this be connected with intelligence or wisdom, or with pollution? — in its more modern sense, the great problem of mankind, what to do with our own garbage.

B. Let me repeat the quotation from Ecclesiasticus — ."Wisdom cometh to the learned man through opportunity for leisure".† A man or woman has to be capable of being learned and can then potentially be wise. We can learn a lot through the experience of having an analysis; when we stop we can also be said to have an opportunity for leisure. To come back to analysis might be an opportunity for clarifying the way to use knowledge. In that way we could become wiser and even have some opportunity for comparing

*"The wisest fool in Christendom" — remark attributed to Henry IV of France about James I of England.

† see p. 90

what we thought we knew a few months or years back with what we know now. Have you tried reading some of the classics to which you were introduced when you were at school? They would appear to remain the same because they are there in print; but do the words, which are the same as the ones you studied at school, have any more meaning?

I suggest the following: Be silent, and as quickly as possible write down what you can observe, either with all your senses about you — that is to say, with your eyes open — or with your eyes shut. Do the same thing again in half an hour, or two hours, or one day, or one week — whatever interval you like — then see if the lists are the same and if the order in which you have written these matters is the same or different. In that way you can compare what you were capable of observing some time ago with what you are capable of observing now. Could you say you were more, or less observant? Could you have any idea about whether you were wiser or not? If you had an idea that you were more observant, but had no idea whether you were wiser, then what is the difference between intelligent observation and wisdom? I am not saying, "Look it up in the dictionary", but I *am* saying, "Look it up in your mind".

Q. You have spoken of rational conjectures about the life of the fetus inside the womb. Would you tell us about one of your clinical experiences?

B. It is useful to me, as a model, if I am shown a photograph of a fetus with its thumb in its mouth; or a fetus that raises its arm as if protecting its eyes. The same thing applies to these conjectures. I find foresight and prudence useful, but I am not a prophet, I am not a seer and I have to make do with rational conjectures. The insightful person or prophet or poet might be able to have much more convincing evidence for behaving with prudence or with foresight. But I have to fall back on these rational and imaginative conjectures. I don't think much of them, but they are the best I have. Similarly in analysis: While I am trying to understand what the analysand is telling me, I have to guess, I have to conjecture until the patient can give me some more convincing evidence; then I may be able to feel reasonably sure of my interpretation.

Q. A writer said, "Life is a product of the conjunction of chemical reactions in intense and continuous movement". In reality we are never the same as we were in the immediately preceding moment. How do you see the temporal nature of the existential being, considering this process of continuous change?

B. Where do the maggots come from in a heap of dead and decaying stuff? How does this heap produce something which is alive and could be called a kind of animal? How would you define the difference between a chair, which seems to be made up of dead matter, and myself who am capable of walking about? What is your definition of the difference between 'dead' objects and 'live' ones? I have never seen any scientific definition of that. A dog would be uninterested in a photograph of another dog; it might smell it, but would show no further interest. But if I show a series of photographs on a screen that dog becomes excited and interested and may want to chase or fight the other dog. Why does it think that a photograph of a dog is uninteresting, but a series of photographs which give the illusion of movement is interesting? We are not in a much better position. In the investigation of life there are more and more elaborate descriptions of the DNA molecule, but we are no nearer, so far as I know, to life.

I suggest that you should ask these questions again next time; I might have become wiser by then. At present I cannot answer them. I don't think there is anything wrong with the questions, but there is a great deal wrong with the answers.

Q. I would like to change the vertex and tell you a story about a psycho-analyst who died and went to Heaven. When he got there he met Saint Peter and showed him his Curriculum Vitae. Saint Peter said he didn't like it. The analyst argued that he had been a good analyst, that he had treated neurotics and psychotics, written books and delivered lectures. Saint Peter said, "You were only looking for promotions and a way to gain access to power. There is no charity or humanity in that. Your fees, too, were quite high". Saint Peter then asked him if he could remember if he had at any time been charitable towards someone. The analyst thought and thought and finally remembered having done a charitable deed. "Oh, I once gave $20.00 to the poor!" Saint Peter then called his assistant Joshua and said, "Give this man $20.00 and show him the way to Hell". The moral of this fable is, "Love is paid with love; money is paid with money". Where, among us psycho-analysts and psychotherapists, does our humanity lie?

B. I don't know. I am afraid that if by some accident — which I think is very unlikely — I got sent to Heaven, there would be masses and masses of sheep, steers, birds, birds that never hatched out of their eggs, all giving evidence that they had been eaten by me. "Dr. Bion, you are at the wrong address. Go back to Hell and get eaten yourself". I do not look forward to an eternity of bliss; enough is enough. In the words of a popular song, "It's love that makes the world go round". A realist looks for sources of energy.

SIX

B. In most scientific disciplines there are material objects to observe, but in the kind of work that we do the problems of observation are different. Even the word 'observation' has to be used by us in a peculiar manner because there is nothing to 'observe' in the way that we observe physical objects. Heisenberg's introduction of the Uncertainty Principle made it clear that even the observation of physical objects is not so simple as it may appear; those difficulties are inescapable when we observe what we call the 'mind'. Nevertheless, we have to observe before we theorize.

Francis Bacon described the possibility of approaching scientific work from above as if one was considering the general principle first and then arguing the existence of supporting evidence. The alternative is to observe the material evidence and then to deduce the general principle from the totality of the observations made. That, he said, is the correct approach. When we have to observe something which has no shape, smell, colour or sound, the problem of evidence — the counterpart of evidence of physical objects — is acute. And yet I do not think it is possible to be engaged on analytic work for long without being convinced that there is a mind. You can observe an animal which is not verbally articulate and yet be convinced that it is thinking. The same thing applies to very young children or even a newly born baby. I was asked yesterday what the clinical evidence was. There cannot be clinical evidence because nobody has analysed a fetus. But it is ridiculous to suppose that a newborn baby has no mind, or that a child of five has a mind but had no mind before infancy or before birth.

In carrying out an analytic investigation we should be aware of the fact that what Melanie Klein described as 'projective identification' takes place even before birth — that is supposing that an embryo can be aware of primordial sensations. If we all became as silent as possible and then noted what we heard in the perfectly silent group, that would give some idea of what the embryo might be aware of. Here again, I have to borrow words from one state of mind and apply them to events in an entirely different state of mind. I find it difficult not to believe in Freud's theory of dreams, but the person who is awake and conscious knows what he saw or heard or experienced in a different state of mind, the state of mind when he was asleep. The person who is awake will believe that he is speaking the truth when he says he had a dream last night. How does he know he had a dream last night? The statement is made by a person who is wide awake; it is a theory of a person who is wide awake about a person who is in the state of mind that he is in when he is asleep.

When we observe a physically mature person is there any evidence of a survival of a different state of mind? Embryologists tell us that there are signs of the survival in the child or grown-up of a branchial cleft. But mature beings don't have branchial clefts; fishes do. A surgeon will say that there is a tumor in the coccyx, the vestigial tail. If that is so, is it not possible that in what we call the 'mind' there are also survivals? And that in certain states of mind these survivals could become apparent if we look in the right 'place'?

I suggest that when we are observing a physically mature person, in no way physically defective, it is possible to be sensitive to behaviour which is somehow peculiar, which does not fit in with what we would consider to be a healthy, normal mind.

I think there is a certain confusion in Freud's ideas of conscious and unconscious. Sometimes he talks about something that is conscious or unconscious; sometimes about a thing that is *in the* conscious — and that is a different idea. The situation I am discussing is one in which the idea of conscious and unconscious is not very illuminating; even the idea of *the* unconscious would be easier to discuss if one thought of it as a thing or place into which you could put something. If, as I suggested before*, the embryo tries to rid itself of unpleasant or unwelcome primordial sensations, it could have 'ideas' or 'feelings' that had *never at any time been conscious*. The nearest I can get to describing it is that these 'ideas' or 'feelings' were 'available' or 'not available'; they have become out of reach of their origin. So when you are dealing with a grown person you will have to distinguish between something that is conscious or unconscious, and something that is *inaccessible*.

What about these dreams? When the patient says he had a dream last night, why does he say so? If he is correct, then the theories of accepted classical psycho-analysis are applicable. However, suppose the patient says that he has no imagination, no dreams. What about that? We may have to consider the possibility that his dreams, his imaginations are not accessible or that he is communicating 'facts'. The patient may take up some athletic activity like wrestling, dancing, gymnastics, eurythmics. But the athletic activity can be a survival of primitive elements of the mind. To fall back on anatomical descriptions, one could say it is a function of the limbic nuclei or other aspects of the basal nuclei.

*see pp. 99, 100

Behaviour which appears to be irrational, or neurotic or hypo chrondriac is much more comprehensible if we think of it as a state in which the unconscious is where the conscious ought to be. Similarly behaviour called 'neurotic' or 'psychotic' can be based on 'facts' unobserved by us. Segal described a patient who talked about a violinist, saying that any fool could see that he was masturbating. The rest of us would think he was playing the violin — not so that patient. The behaviour of certain patients — a smile for instance — is misleadingly similar to that of neurotics, hypochondriacs, or even a baby who is thought to be smiling because it has 'wind'. The expression on the faces of a piece of Etruscan funeral sculpture is sometimes called an 'archaic smile'; it appears to mean the same as a smile on any ordinary countenance, but it is not. I have known a man treated as a criminal for what in the army was called 'dumb insolence'; it is a mistaken interpretation. A psychiatrist would call it a sympton of schizophrenia, but I am not sure that that interpretation is good enough as far as psycho-analysts are concerned. We have to observe what the patient says to us, the flow of blood in his cheeks, or the lack of blood in his cheeks, or the movement of his muscles. Sometimes we can see peculiar movements in the voluntary musculature; sometimes there can be movement of involuntary muscle. Although these movements of involuntary muscle can be betrayed on the X-ray screen if the patient has a barium meal, this kind of apparatus is not available in a psycho-analytic consultation; we have to learn a new way to observe.

Q. What are the causes of the inhibition of adequate thinking? Laziness? Search for ease? Or emotion?

B. There can be all those causes, but I am not sure that it is illuminating to consider the obstacles alone. However you want to express something in yourself — as a composer of music, or as a sculptor or a writer — all these approaches are difficult, partly because so many of the earliest years are spent in trying to get rid of who you are. As you say, there is an inhibition, an obstruction. A child tries to be good, tries to be who or what he thinks his father or mother wants him to be; a great deal of time is spent in trying to be *not* himself or herself. It is therefore hard to change to wanting to express who you are; it is like changing the direction of your thought. A sculptor can try to tell people who are not him or her self something they have not noticed hitherto by making a trap for light. Having made such a trap there has to be somebody who wants to look at it, but that person is more used to looking at the piece of stone than at the shape of the light. Similarly, a painter can depict something with his pigments on canvas; those pigments and that flat surface can trap light. So you can see a portrait painted by Picasso and fail to see what is drawn or painted on the canvas. You can say, "It doesn't look like any human face that I see". Nor does a sculpture by Rodin look like a statue such as the David by Michelangelo, or the Hermes portrayed by Praxiteles; they were portraying something in a different way. A writer may use words in a way which is not the same as the way in which they have so far been used. James Joyce said you ought to spend your life in reading Finnegan's Wake, and then you might understand what he means. The shape which is expressed by his words is different from the shape which is expressed by the words of, say, Shakespeare or Milton.

Artists have a way of expressing themselves which changes painting or sculpture or writing into something new. Perhaps Shakespeare himself couldn't understand one of his own plays performed today. Or if Freud were able to come back he wouldn't understand psycho-analysis. These people do something to the human mind which means that it is never the same again. So the question is not so much what the inhibitions are, but what the person wants to pass on. What he does *not* want to pass on, what he wants to *in*hibit, is only a part of what he is trying to *ex*hibit.

Q. I would like you to explain how you perceive the so-called psycho-somatic illnesses.

B. I don't think that my explanation matters. What I would draw attention to is the *nature* of the problem. For example: This (the palm of the hand) is a representation of the psycho-somatic illness. Now watch: This (the back of the hand) is the soma-psychotic illness. It is the same hand; it is the same complaint. Looked at from one side it is psycho-somatic; come round to the other side and you will see the soma-psychotic. Putting it into other words, if you don't feel satisfied at seeing a psycho-somatic illness, change your vertex and look at it from the other side. The same thing with the inhibition: Look at it from one side and it says "No"; look at it from the other side and it says "Yes".

Q. I would like you to clarify certain attacks made by the patient on the analyst by the use of strong suicidal emotions.

B. The patient may be capable of arousing powerful feelings in the analyst. He can make me afraid that he will commit suicide; or he can make me feel love or hate. My ability to think clearly can easily be destroyed by a patient who plays on my emotions. While the analyst can say things which play on the patient, the patient can equally play on the analyst. The problem for the analyst, or any other doctor, is how to help somebody who can stop him from thinking clearly. He can try to make it easier for the patient to think clearly; but the patient may not want to make it easier for the analyst to think clearly. A terrorist can terrify two people who want to discuss a problem — so the terrorist wins. The minimum conditions for discussion are destroyed because terror is not a state of mind which is conducive to clear thinking. The terrorist is able to mobilize fundamental and powerful feelings, feelings which are often expressed in a sophisticated manner as fighting or running away. But neither the activity of fighting nor the activity of running away is easily harmonized with thinking clearly. Terrorism is the weapon, the prerogative of the mentally deficient.

SEVEN

B. I have suggested that the potentially intelligent fetus resorts to a mechanism analogous to what Melanie Klein describes post-natally as 'projective identification'. These primordial germs of thought and feeling become inaccessible — that is to say, out of reach and control of what will later be the character or personality. That state of mind, as soon as the embryo or fetus can be said to have a mind, is different from that of the infant who displays thought and behaviour to which these concepts of conscious and unconscious are applicable. The infant or child who shows unconscious mechanisms and who behaves as if it had an unconscious does seem to experience some kind of ceasura which Rank called the 'birth trauma'. In other words, there is a continuity between the full-term fetus and the infant although the continuity is both maintained and broken by what appears to be a synapse, or diaphragm, or screen, so that the primordial thought of the fetus is projected onto this caesura and is reflected back from the infant to its primordial levels of thought and feeling. There is a contact through this permeable membrane in both directions; the caesura is a transparent mirror. The infant or child can experience feelings which seep up from the unconscious and which can similarly be affected in the opposite direction. That is to say, the thought of the infant or child can affect these primitive levels of behaviour. This is different from the state of affairs which exists in the embryonic growth of what we would later expect to be its mind. The separation of these two powers of thought is much more nearly complete, but a puzzling situation is produced because it does not *appear* to be like that. This same genetically gifted creature is able to start, *as if after birth*, to learn how to behave exactly like everybody else. At first one would suppose that this organism is highly intelligent, can learn easily and is able to compete successfully with its brothers and sisters. It is therefore something of a surprise when at one of the periods of emotional turmoil such as adolescence, or latency which is another period of turbulence marked by apparent calm, peculiar kinds of behaviour start appearing. The child suddenly seems to be incapable of understanding or behaving in a common sense way; he behaves as if he had no common sense at all. Conversely, when one expects bizarre behaviour he behaves in a logical way. I mentioned an example of this when I quoted the case of the patient who said that anybody knows that the violinist is masturbating in public.* In analysis it would be a long time before you were able to show a musician, or a patient who could play the violin, that he was using statements about playing the violin as a method of expressing unconscious, masturbatory desires. Thus, on the one hand there is the neurotic to whom it is difficult to demonstrate the existence of unconscious impulses, masturbatory activities and so on; on the other hand, the intelligent person who seems to be unable to appreciate beautiful violin playing, but has no difficulty whatsoever in seeing that the violinist is masturbating.

I think that there is some connection between this latter kind of personality — whom I will call, for convenience, 'psychotic' — and the one that I call 'neurotic'; between the psychotic mental activity and rational or socially acceptable behaviour. It seems to be accepted that the neurotic's ordinary, social, commonsense thinking has a psychotic base. This is what I think Melanie Klein means when she refers to the depressive position and the paranoid schizoid position; she is referring to levels of thinking and feeling which in isolation would be called 'psychotic'. She argues that the neurotic individual cannot be considered to be analysed until these psychotic elements have been displayed.

It is convenient to consider the psychotic patient as also being divisible, as being an 'insane' psychotic in contrast with a 'sane' psychotic. I am using the terms 'sane' and 'insane' with an emphasis on the Latin origins — 'healthy' and 'unhealthy'. The sane psychotic has vestiges of rational, conscious behaviour; something can be done to develop them. The insane psychotic, on the other hand, finds his way into a psychiatric hospital and usually deteriorates there.

*see p. 106

What are you dealing with when somebody comes to your consulting room and wants an analysis? Is there any way in which you could formulate to yourself what category of person you think you are dealing with? It is not only an academic point because on the answer to that question depends whether you want to see the patient or not. That is something you have to decide almost at once. Indeed, one can say that you have to decide in haste and repent at leisure.

You may get a clue if you consider the caesura as a mental diaphragm. When you see your patient, how easily can you mentally change your position, your vertex, so that you can almost see both sides?

If you feel disposed to analyse an asthmatic patient you will very soon find yourself in the kind of trouble that I can describe from an actual experience.

The patient is admitted to a medical ward as a case of asthma. The analyst sees the patient there, possibly in a ward with screens drawn round the bed, or possibly in a small sub-ward in which the analyst and patient are alone together. Within two or three sessions the patient's asthma gets worse. So far so good; nobody minds that because they think that asthmatic patients tend to have these relapses. But further progress in the analysis releases the patient's capacity for mobilizing the opinion of the ward. And the analyst finds his appearance is the signal for marked disapproval from all the inhabitants of the ward. It becomes clear that their sympathies are in support of the poor patient who is being so foolishly and unkindly talked to by the analyst. The patient, who may have been regarded as a bit of a nuisance, is now more generally regarded as a person of charm and intelligence. There is only one real defect — his addiction to psycho-analysis. People cannot understand why such a nice man, such a gifted man, has that peculiar habit of going to see an analyst. In the course of the analytic sessions the patient can let drop an increasing number of unpleasing comments. He says that while he is determined to go on with the analysis, so-an-so, who is a very intelligent women, cannot think why he is so foolish as to go to that horrible doctor who clearly has no qualifications and is a stupid, unscrupulous money-maker. He talks more and more of his unfortunate experience of having to put up with these hostile comments about his analyst whom he so much admires. Further progress in the analysis leads to a situation in which the patient who has never experienced frustration, who has never had any fears of insanity and who has never been physically ill, now begins to catch colds, now begins to be afraid that he is going mad, begins to be unpopular, even has the impulse — which he has never had before — to commit suicide. —

The state I have just described is remarkably reminiscent of that in which these primordial ailments are inaccessible, have never been conscious, because they have been got rid of *at source*. At a much later age these things which have been inaccessible, which have never been unconscious, which have never been conscious, now become both. The fear of suicide ceases to be a fear; it comes much nearer to a reality, making the threat of suicide dangerous. The patient will resist discussion of the impulse to commit suicide; he will mention it, but does not want to talk any more about it, If the analyst persists then be becomes responsible for putting thoughts of suicide into the patient's mind. I think it is a good thing, before you see such a patient, to arrange your room so that you could interpose between a sudden impulse of that kind and the action which he can take quickly and suddenly. There is no real intervening phase between the expressed impulse or fear and its translation into action. Thus the stage is set for instantaneous catastrophy.

It is not much good hospitalizing such a patient; there is no alternative to going on with the analysis — or none that I know of. This patient has never had the experience — which most people have had — of being afraid of insanity, afraid of masturbation, afraid of sex, fundamentally afraid that he is going mad or will go mad one day. So he comes to this fear without any of the preliminary experience of fear of it. It is, therefore, a tremendous shock to feel afraid of going mad *and* to feel that he is quite right — that in fact he has already gone mad. It is almost like throwing yourself out of the window and finding in mid-air that you have committed suicide; it is too late.

Q. Would you say something more about the 'psycho-analytic calendar', the way in which one can date an occurrence between the patient and his analyst?

B. I think the question is related to this matter of 'vertex'; something which is not clear can become clear if you move off to one side or the other. For example, you can ask yourself what a problem would look like if you were an Elizabethan, or if you were one of the early settlers in South America. It can often give you a clue as to the nature of that problem when discussion seems to be at an end and further inspection from one standpoint yields no further result.* The same thing can be done by changing, not so much your geographical position, but your position in time. You can look at the matter as if you were using the second hand of a watch. If you were timing an Olympic runner over a distance of a hundred yards you

*In the Mahabharata 'dates' are virtually ignored. In psycho-analysis we talk about the past or the future. What the evidence is for such spontaneous dating is not yet clear.

would have to use a watch which recorded split seconds; if it was a marathon run then the watch would have to be a different one. If you were discussing verbal communication the scale would probably have to be tens of thousands of years; if you were discussing the length of time that human life itself has existed on the earth you would have to use a time scale of hundreds of thousands of years. If you were considering where this building would be by the time the spiral nebula of which we are part had rotated enough to carry us to the opposite side of the nebula, then you would have to measure that in terms of cosmic time, in terms of 10^8 million light years. It is useful to accustom oneself to these imaginative vertices of thought. If we are discussing civilized thought or behaviour we have to consider a time scale measuring the distance between the height of Egyptian civilization and the present day; if an archaeologist is excavating the remains of Mohenjo Daro he has to find some method by which he can place it in the calendar of human history. But supposing you have before you a patient who is a civilized, educated human being and something appears or is uncovered which is curiously anomalous — such as a statement that anybody knows that a violinist is masturbating. How do you date that fragment?

I had the experience in war of discussing with two or three of my friends the feeling that we did not want to go on fighting, that warfare seemed to be ridiculous and stupid. That discussion was extraordinarily similar to another which is clearly described in the Bhagavadgita where Arjuna argues with Krishna and says, "These opponents include many of my best friends, many people whom I admire, who are relatives of mine"; he throws down his weapons and says, "I will not fight".

Many of today's problems expressed by our patients can be recognized as having been problems from the beginnings of recorded time. It is useful, therefore, to have at your disposal your own particular framework, your own psychological architectonic, so that if you are trying to portray the mind with which you are in contact you can date various parts of it according to an already prepared scheme, a grid of your own construction. The Grid which I drew up needs to be improved by you for your own use; it is merely an indication of the kind of thing which might be an aid. The time dimension, which can be measured by watches or clocks or calendars, is only one co-ordinate enabling you to place a finding in space. If you use a large scale then psycho-analysis occupies only a very small part up to the present; it is only a recent off-shoot of the capacity for thought. But the capacity for thinking is itself only a recent bi-product of the development of what we are used to considering as human life. And that in turn is only a relatively recent phenomenon in terms of the development of live objects—plants and viruses as well as animals.

Q. In the sixteenth century Tome de Souza decreed that for every person eaten by cannibal-Indians an Indian would be shot from a cannon. Thus the whole of the cannibal-Indian culture was destroyed along with cannibalism. What happens to the patient if his destructiveness is 'killed' by the analytic work?

B. The human animal must in fact be extremely destructive because we still exist, we have been able to destroy all our foes such as the animals which might want to eat us. We are still at it; we are still trying to destroy spirochetes, gonnoccochi, minute creatures. But we are also dependent on our fellows. How are we to adjust to 'civilized' life, namely, being part of a civil community? We have to become adjusted to a herd existence, but while there is an impulse to live co-operatively with our fellow animals, at the same time there is an impulse to band together to wage war against another collection of people. There is an impulse to say, "*This* animal looks the same and has the same smell as I have, so I'll get together with it. *That* animal, on the other hand, has a different colour and a different smell — let's kill it". Terms like 'The United Kingdom', 'The United States', and now 'The United Nations', are premature and precocious. Just how united we are we can see by having a close-up look at these various united states; we usually find that they show every sign of disintegrating. What are we to make of this paradoxical development? For how long could we say that there is a state of unification in the journey from barbarism to decay? For how long could we say that any society of people is civilized between the time when it is barbarian and the time when it is in decay? Sometimes it looks as if a nation goes from barbarism to decay with virtually no phase of civilization between. Of course it does depend on how you define 'civilized behaviour'. In some respects we attach great importance to works of art if a society produces the kind of grave furniture found in the tomb of Tutenkhamun. I read recently of a woman who was buried, in accordance with her wishes, seated at the wheel of her Ferrari motor car. What a fascinating archaeological discovery that will be! How should we date the artistic achievements of *that* civilization?

8

EIGHT

B. Hitherto we have been discussing matters for which I think there is very little, if any, scientific evidence. A hostile critic could easily say, "This is all pure imagination". I would say, "Yes but I think it is time that 'pure imagination' was recognized as having a place in scientific work. If that is considered to be exclusive we had better reconsider a great deal of what passes for scientific work so that we may be quite sure that some of these extremely prestigious papers could not be classified more adequately as 'science fiction' than as scientific work — in the sense of formulations of the truth to which they are pretending to aspire".

I think it is fair to assume that when a patient comes to us he sincerely means to speak the truth, but he may be unaware of the great difficulties involved. However, *we* should be aware of those difficulties and should not claim a higher status for our theories than is justified by a critical appreciation. Otherwise we could find ourselves trying to defend the indefensible.

To turn now from imaginative conjectures and rational conjectures to something for which I would claim rather more credibility. The language and theories of psycho-analysis are swept more and more into the domains of social discussion. I remember, when I was first at medical school, one used to hear socially about Father Figures, Oedipus Situations and the rest of what I can only call Freud's tomb furniture dug out of Freud's works. It sounded plausible and even learned. Today I think it has become still more widespread. We are all familiar with psycho-analysis which is much 'improved' but which is in fact based on an inadequate understanding of psycho-analytic theories. I think the instincts of psycho-analytic societies are right when so much emphasis is placed on individual psycho-analysis.

I want to draw your attention to a peculiar and doubtful situation which no single analyst can fully investigate — one doesn't live long enough. But if all of us are sensitive to it then between us we may be able to make some progress in this 'obscure domain'.

The patient lies down on the couch and starts off without the slightest hesitation by saying he had a dream last night. I don't want

to give the impression that I think he is lying, or that I don't
believe him; at the same time I would not assume that that statement
is a true one. I would be alert to the possibility that what I am being
told is not correctly described by the patient as 'a dream', however
sincere he is. Is there any way in which one can be sensitive to the
possibility that one is not listening to a dream? Are there any
'facts' in the actual practice of psycho-analysis which make one
wonder what one is listening to?

While the patient is telling me his dream I find myself wondering
why he should take the trouble to dream it. The account is so literal;
it doesn't sound like an imagination; it sounds as if it might easily
have happened. That is a subjective criterion; it depends on the
feeling that, having listened to a great number of dreams, there is a
difference in them which is not simply due to the fact that we are all
different individuals and that therefore no two dreams are likely
to be the same or even similar. My suspicions are aroused if the
dream is recounted without any hesitation, no groping for recollec-
tions, great detail and a similarity to an ordinary story. One of my
earliest experiences of this was with a patient who started telling
me a dream at the beginning of the session and went on and on.
I began to feel, "I wish he would get on with it —I shan't have any
time to interpet this". The patient may have been trying to deny me
time for an interpretation but I did not think so. I contained my
impatience and went on listening. And he *did* go on to the end of the
session. Finally I had to say, "Well, we'll have to leave that for the
present". I think the patient was a bit suspicious that I had not
listened to the entire account and surprised when I said it was time
to stop and hadn't given him any interpretation at all.

At the next session he said, "You didn't give me any interpretation". I said, "Perhaps if you go on with the dream we may have
time for interpretation today, or perhaps next time". He said he
couldn't. But I was prepared to believe that he could go on with that
'dream'; I felt that he had been disconcerted by my invitation to
continue. However, he then went on with free associations as any
person who was having an analysis might do. But I did not feel that
he was wide awake or that he was continuing with conscious communications. I could put it this way: I thought he was continuing in
a different state of mind; a state of mind in which a person is when
they are what we call 'awake'; the state of mind in which people are
when they are aware that it is daylight. Conversely, the alleged
dream is a reminiscence of the state of mind of a person when asleep
and probably when it is dark. (Gerard Manley Hopkins wrote,
"I wake and feel the fell of dark". "The fell of dark" is a term, somewhat ambiguously used, with an uncommon meaning of 'fell', that is,

'pelt' or 'fur'. So the quotation also means, 'I wake and feel darkness as if it were an animal skin'.)

It sounds as if the patient had a dream last night and it would be reasonable to interpret it according to what one knows about dreams. But the dream that the patient is reporting is different. It has something about it that makes me feel that if I had had that dream then I could feel it in the way I could feel a fur coat.

I don't pay a great deal of attention to the fact that when the patient says he had that dream and recounts it he is awake and apparently in the state of mind in which people call the nocturnal experience 'a dream'. I cannot say that he is hallucinated or deluded; it would be much more satisfactory if I could but I don't want to give you any idea of certainty about it. I would leave you sensitive to events of this peculiar nature so that when they occur in your consulting room you can make your own contribution to what it is that is happening.

I have referred elsewhere to a statement made by Blanchot— "La réponse est le malheur de la question"—which might be translated, "The answer is the misfortune or disease of curiosity". In other words, nothing kills curiosity so thoroughly as the answer. A patient who keeps on saying, every time you give an interpretation, "Yes I know, yes I know, yes I know", or "I don't know what you mean", kills further curiosity. You cannot continue to research into that matter; the patient already knows all the answers; or, alternatively, he doesn't understand any answer you give. He equally doesn't know any answer that *he* would give, so both people are in the same unfortunate position. He cannot be analysed; I cannot analyse. To borrow Milton's phrase, "Wisdom at one entrance quite shut out". That sort of behaviour on the part of the patient makes it impossible for you to use your senses; it hurts to listen to it. It is similar to the situation which arises with the patient who says he has no imagination; the patient who says he has a dream and tells you the sort of dream I have just described; the patient who fatigues and deafens your ears so that you cannot listen to what he says. If I try to summarize that situation I could say that the patient is disturbed, or a borderline psychotic. I would have told you precisely nothing. To try to tell you something more positive I fall back on more imaginative conjecture. I suggest that this same patient is a very good practising psycho-analyst of the sort that detects all my weak points and knows exactly how to play on them. If he knows from what he can see or feel about me that there are certain sounds which I find difficult to tolerate—like "Yes I know", "I mean-to-say", "You know", "I don't understand what you mean"—then he can bombard me with those statements; he can innoculate me with that kind of verbal soporific.

As in Hamlet, poison can be poured into the ear so that one's analytic capacity is destroyed. Such a patient, if successful, leaves you a worse analyst at the end of his treatment than you were when you first met. I do not mean that this is consciously deliberate — it is 'a gift'.

These discussions seem to be disjointed because in the practice of analysis the disjointed nature of the evidence is part of the difficulty. You may have bits of evidence which are scattered over the material of a period of some months or more and it is not easy to see that the bits are related to each other. It is particularly difficult because you cannot exclude the possibility that their connection may be in your own mind and not proper to the material.

I want to talk now about one of these instances of what I have called the patient's restlessness. He may talk of having taken up classical dancing, gymnastics, or there may be something more immediately noticeable, namely, his posture on the couch or his wish to change from the couch to the chair, or from one chair to another. It is often unobtrusive. Sometimes the patient may call attention to himself without appreciating the significance of the fact to which he is calling attention. He will laugh or make a joke of it, and may not like it when he finds that you take it seriously. The important point is the fact that the patient is beginning to want to make athletic rather than verbal communication. If, in the formulations which we use as free associations, the patient can give expression to the symptoms, the complaints of which he is aware, then perhaps it is possible that we can use the same channel of communication in the *opposite direction*. Can we communicate something verbally to the patient so that he can transmit it through his central nervous system, through the ramifications of the autonomic and the sympathetic systems to the address to which we want it to go? If the patient is delivering his communication to you through a system which comes to the surface in a form which we recognize —asthma for example — is it possible to communicate with such a patient so that the interpretation goes through his lungs back to wherever the origin of the asthma lies? In physical medicine we could say we might hope to examine a patient physically and find where we thought the focus of infection lay. Could we find some method by which our interpretation found its way back to the point of origin of what we think is a mental system, like a symptom of anxiety or dread, or terror or panic fear. Frequently a seriously disturbed patient has spent his life in denying any expression to what he suspects is a serious disorder — the sort of thing we could call a psychosis or mania. It is too often forgotten that the seriously disturbed patient is being disturbed because he is aware of something serious, even if his analyst isn't, and does not want to be reminded of it. Analyst and analysand can be at one in wishing to deprecate the seriousness of 'mental pain'— hence a dangerous collusion.

The patient is likely to express his terrifying feelings and experiences in terms which are deceptively faint and unspectacular. So when you hear a patient jokingly refer to having taken up dancing or other physical activity could you find some method by which to communicate through that same system which has shown itself by this faint and hardly perceptible comment?

At the present time I think it is probably wiser to keep to the ordinary, conventional system of verbal communication, to give interpretations as accurately and as artistically as we can. I say 'artistically' because I don't think it is much good producing more and more psycho-analytic journals and papers to a point where we fatigue the eyes of readers. When a new Journal is announced do you feel that your "heart leaps up with joy"? Or do you feel disposed to cancel your subscription? If the latter then I suggest that you don't write any more articles like that yourself. It is easy to say, but it is in fact difficult not to write the same tedious and inartistic language oneself. I don't in any way claim exemption from the complaint, but I do think that we ought to try to express ourselves so that it is a pleasure for the recipient to receive. Artists can say disagreeable and frightening things; yet we may be prepared to listen to their music, read their books or look at their sculptures.

Q.1. Is there any difference between a somatic and a hypochondriac delirium?

B. Yes, if you think so. What that difference is has to be determined by the validation of the psycho-analyst in the experience while it takes place.

Q.2. What would be their clinical and psychodynamic aspects?

B. I should have thought that the 'somatic delirium' refers to the total soma; if it is 'hypochondriac' then I would be inclined to think that it is only related to that part of the soma which is below the chondria. A term like 'hypochondriac' has been so abused that it has come to mean that the person *is* hypochondriac and therefore there is nothing the matter with him. *If* he is hypochondriac, and that is a correct description, then one ought to pay serious attention to that localization.

In English we talk about a 'sweet heart'. [Translated as 'noivo'] No, I didn't say that Portuguese word; I said "a sweet heart". I think a Chinese could say, as a term of endearment, "my heart and liver", meaning a beloved girl-friend or boy-friend. Why these anatomical descriptions? Is it hypochondriac love or somatic love? Ought we to attach more importance to these statements? They are meant seriously by the people who use them. Unfortunately words like 'love' have become so debased that it is difficult for people who *do* love each other to know what language to use or what attention to pay to anybody who addresses them in such terms. Why is it that when somebody says "I love you" to you, you sometimes feel that it is a very important statement that has been made, but at other times you pay no more attention to it than you would to an advertisement for a brand of cereal? There must be something of which you are aware which makes you know that those same words have fundamentally and basically different values according to their context. That is why in analysis it is so important to be aware of the context in which the words, whatever they are, are spoken.

I often feel that I have to listen to the patient for a long time and don't feel disposed to interrupt and break his train of thought. but if I say nothing because I want to listen, that fact itself can act as an interruption; the patient can say, "Doctor, have you gone to sleep?" The patient is familiar with the fact that people who apparently are listening and paying attention are in fact absent in mind.

A bore, a gifted bore, can leave you no choice except to be absent in mind and then say, "Doctor, are you asleep?" To which one is tempted to reply, "Well, if I'm not, why not?" It is a subtle form of cruelty to be able to be a bore and to demand full attention of the boredom. So instead of making that somewhat frivolous reply it might be better to consider the matter and to draw the patient's attention to the subtle pleasures of cruelty and the experience of being cruelly treated; it is a primitive and basic form of sexual love, and therefore something that requires attention.

NINE

B. We consider that the human individual behaves exactly as if it had some kind of will, or purpose, or government. In the study of the individual cell, individual person who has boundaries which are the same as the boundaries of his body, an attempt has been made to describe that body with names like 'hand', 'arm', 'head' and so on. But once the anatomists and physiologists look into the matter they tell us that they don't know what is meant by 'a hand' because they don't know where the hand starts and where it finishes. We could carry out violent investigations by cutting off a hand or a foot, but it is noticeable that the human cell or individual is never the same when these violent operations are carried out — and the change is striking indeed if you cut off the head. In fact the popular idea is that the dead person is very different from the live one.

That is a relatively simple problem, but anatomists know of 'ghost hands', 'ghosts' of such portions of the body that have been removed. We understand that there is an obvious explanation in the continued stimulation of the nerve endings which previously went to the missing organ. The psycho-analyst's problem is that he is told of pains which cannot be linked with physical structures; we call them 'mental pains'.

The problem exists in part because there is no adequate or satisfactory geography or map of the human mind. Perhaps that is because there is no such thing — it may be a figment of the imagination. But it does look as if the idea that the mind is in some way subject to the same limitations, the same boundaries as the body, can no longer be regarded as true. Through the use of the vocal cords the human creature can communicate with other individuals; the characteristics of one individual can be spread to other individuals.

It becomes clear that attempts to describe the mind — soul, supersoul, for example — are not adequate. Freud suggested the terms id, ego, superego. The Jesuits described an 'arbitrium' which has a function which betrays itself as arbitrating between one part of the mind and another. The problem is open-ended; the more we investigate it the more we have to revise existing theories.

Human individuals are also creatures which hunt in packs or herds and which have many of the characteristics of agglomeration — they form towns and cities. But so do insects like termites and ants who build up extraordinary structures and behave as if they were joined to each other. Fishes, whales, dolphins — they all have a method of communication, as well as those animals that have given up the water medium and have taken to the air. Flying birds seem to move and wheel together; at other times they form what looks like a pattern to us who are engaged on crawling about the surface of the earth. The pointed end of the pattern, a wedge shape, is occupied by a succession of individuals, constantly changing. How is that done? Is the leader giving orders to the entire flight? Or is the leader representing the direction in which the flight is to go? (I use this model to represent the problem of the mind; who or what decides the course the individual should take?) I think that there is a barrier, a caesura, between my kind of animal and that kind of animal, and between ourselves and ourselves. As far as we are concerned, because we are so close to the crowd of us it becomes difficult to see any pattern at all.

In my attempts to investigate the mind, character, personality or individual, I believe that it is possible to see a certain pattern that is not the same as the pattern of the physical body. Sometimes I can detect a curious state in which the individual is what I have to call 'highly intelligent'. I have to borrow these words from various disciplines for which they were invented, to use them for a different discipline — the discipline which is involved in investigating this mind which we suppose exists. I think I can detect people who are so intelligent, who know so much, that the knowledge is too thick to be able to discern the wisdom. It sounds like a paradox; they are too intelligent to be wise.* Such people seem to be able to become technically proficient. For example, I have spoken before of the person who can be a technically proficient violinist, but is incapable of being a musician.

So far the human animal has been very successful; its achievements are extraordinary. A quadruped learns to perform athletic feats like walking on two hind legs; it then goes on to increasingly complex technical activities — sexual activities, for example. The individual graduates from the simple discovery of pleasurable sensations on its own body to similar activities which are carried out by two individuals. Religiously trained people talk about two people becoming one, a process which you could call 'at-one-ment'. The more usual pronunciation in English is 'atonement'; the alphabetic letters are the same whether it is 'at-one-ment' or 'atonement'; they are put together in the same order, but they are not the same word. It has been said that 'at-one-ment' is my invention. I say it isn't. Who will be the arbiter?

*see also p. 101

Someone may ask, "What is the result of the examination? What have you found out after your mental dissection of the human mind?" I can only say that this same investigation, carried out by myself with the help of another self — which is usually the patient — seems to promote growth or development. Therefore the true investigation is a treatment as well as a cure. The discussion is not something dramatic, like capital punishment; a quick solution is always something drastic and apparently finite. A final solution appears to be quick; real solutions require time.

The finite leaves no room for development; we are concerned with something which does require space for growth.

To illustrate some of the problems which face us all I take as a method of description a large scale operation — the plight of the 14th British Army which was defeated at Rangoon in 1942. The British in Singapore had previously detached two battle cruisers to support the garrison. Both those battleships, the latest weapons with which the Royal Navy was armed, were destroyed by Japanese dive bombers. The blow was a serious one; the 14th British Army was thrown back in disorder with hardly any arms, weapons or even boots to wear. And there it was besieged — the remnants — at Imphal.

There was introduced as commander of the besieged forces a civilian who had joined the Territorial Cadets — a step which was strongly disapproved of by his fellow civilians. However, he liked that voluntary soldiering and became a regular army officer. He saw service in the desert and in the war against the German forces. Much to his annoyance and disgust he was withdrawn and sent to India where he was again withdrawn and sent to command the remnants of the British Army in Imphal.

It was not an enviable post to be put in command of the remnants of a dispirited, demoralized and defeated army. But this civilian-turned-soldier told his fellow troops that if they were cut off from their base, if the enemy had surrounded Imphal — as indeed it had — so these remnants of the 14th Army could equally be said to have cut off the Japanese from Japan. It was only an idea of course, only an imaginative fiction. However, the character or spirit or soul infected this decayed and destroyed remnant of an army with health. The *idea*, the fiction that the 14th non-existent British Army had cut off the Japanese forces from Japan, started becoming a reality. The British could get no more equipment from Britain because Britain couldn't be bothered with what happened in faraway places like Burma. So they had to march; I don't know what they marched on — their bare feet were hardly enough. It is difficult to say they marched on their morale or on their spirit which had been produced by the injection of this amateur-turned-professional called General Slim.

The Japanese had discovered the secret British code so that they could read all the messages which the army commander communicated to his troops. General Slim, who had a habit of thinking, decided to go on using the same code. Through this code, which he knew the Japanese could now understand, he continued to transmit messages to his left flank. The Japanese naturally concentrated their troops against the left flank of what was a non-existent army — another figment of the imagination.

When the Japanese had concentrated their troops against this non-existent left flank, the remnants of the 14th Army, now reinforced by the spirit of General Slim, broke through the weakened Japanese left flank and defeated the Japanese who had nothing to fight but the air. While they were busy fighting a figment of General Slim's imagination the real remnants of the 14th Army found themselves in Rangoon receiving the surrender of the Japanese commander.

What are we to say about this 'spirit', this 'soul' or 'mind'? That is what we are supposed to be dealing with. Does it exist, or does it not? Are we concerned with a figment of our imagination, or is there something behind these words?

I don't know the answers to these questions — I wouldn't tell you if I did. I think it is important to find out for yourselves. When you go to your consulting rooms tomorrow perhaps you will investigate this matter, and perhaps between us we may ultimately find out what this thing is that had no shape or taste or colour, or anything that our senses can make us aware of. At the same time perhaps you will find out what it is that *you* use to get in touch with this other invisible self. It seems to me that it is real enough to leave room for the development of this 'thing' of which my senses give me no knowledge and for which I cannot find any language with which to communicate it to you.

Who or what breathes spirit into a collection of people and makes them develop? What shape will the Brazilian nation take? What shape could we see if we could see it in the way that we see the shape of a flight of birds? Our view is close up, microscopic, a small part of the whole; what is the real pattern?

Milton, by means of the 'Areopagitica'*, tried to infuse his ideas into his countrymen; today we can see more of what his ideas were, what happened to them, what happened to his countrymen. Who or what will lead this collection to which we are too near to see and of which we are one 'cell'? The question could equally be posed about the individual who is a group of thoughts and feelings.

* A Speech for the Liberty of Unlicenced Printing

Are there too many Brazilians for us to be able to see the Brazilian nation? Perhaps somebody who can will write it down, or compose it musically, or paint it. Or form it into a conglomeration which, like an army, has a structure.

The past is mostly forgotten, the future we cannot see, but is there some seer who could detect the germs of the future? What is a psycho-analyst? What does he do? what has he become? The answer is the disease of, ultimately the destruction of, curiosity. But in the mean-time the question itself may provoke growth.

TEN

B. One of the questions which analysts have often not asked themselves is, "Do I want to be a psycho-analyst?" Men and women have problems that they think are going to be 'cured'; so they go to see an analyst to 'get cured'. The question of embracing the psycho-analytic profession is not considered. It is assumed that they *can* be analysts and that therefore they *want* to be. But it is an open-ended question worth constantly asking yourself. There are other versions of it: Do you want to be a particular person's analyst? Would you like to have another patient? Would you like to have another patient like the last one? You can consider which of the patients that you ever had are the ones with whom you have had the most rewarding experience. It can be something of a surprise to find which are the ones you find most rewarding and what sort of person *you* must be to like that kind of patient. That is another reason for regarding the question as open-ended; you do not *stop* learning something about yourself.

If your central nervous system is in tolerable working order then your senses give you a lot of information. After that what you think that information means is up to you. But that depends on whether you want to know the meaning; you may not. Similarly, there are patients who get a 'nice' sensation from the sound of your voice and possibly from the sound of their own. So analyst and analysand settle into a meaningless debate because it feels so 'nice'. The patient feels something which is analogous in physical terms to being stroked; the one mind has a caressing, soothing effect on the other and the mutually gratifying seduction goes on unobserved by either party — so much so that it is forgotten that the patient has come for help. The patient has forgotten it; the analyst has forgotten it; they are locked in a mutually gratifying experience.

It may be a long time before the patient becomes aware of discomfort. It is as if he had access to some soporific drug so that he cannot tell you where the pain is. Here again it is useful to change the vertex so that if you cannot see the pain from one position you may be able to see it from another.

Sometimes the story that is told you is comprehensible but not illuminating; it may then be useful to consider what is wrong with the story. Why does the patient think it is worth while spending time and money telling you that story? Why does he think that you might be interested to hear it? For example, a patient who has been going to the analyst for five or six years goes to a hospital for a physical examination, tells them something that the analyst has been analysing from the point of view of its being a hypochondriacal symptom, and is told that he has a terminal illness. The patient asks for an interview with the analyst or perhaps he asks the analyst to come to the hospital to see him there. The analyst comes into the ward and finds the patient undergoing some form of elaborate treatment for the complaint. The patient pours out a mass of abuse on the grounds that the analyst has been treating the illness as a hypo chondriacal symptom. "If", says the patient, "you knew your job, that symptom could have been treated properly long before it became a hopeless terminal case". As the analyst looks at all the apparatus there is no reason to doubt the truth of the statement that the patient's condition is hopeless; that would seem to be all there was to say about it. What is wrong with that story?

I will give you some idea of how my mind would work on this problem. I don't say it would suit anybody else, but it may help you to find the way that would suit you.

If it is true that the patient is suffering from a terminal illness time is short; therefore the best use needs to be made of what is left. If I felt that I was going to die shortly I don't think I would want to waste my time telling a psycho-analyst what a fool he was — I think I would leave him to find that out for himself. So why, out of the small supply of time which is available, should the patient want to see me as the analyst? Either he is being extremely prodigal in the use of the time, or there is some other reason for wanting to see me. What other reason could there be? If the patient feels that I have simply been telling him a series of ridiculously untrue stories, he could hardly be wanting to hear more of the same. On the other hand, if, as is the case with this particular patient, he has been told stupid and false stories for a long time, he may want to hear the truth. The story that it is a terminal illness is true but irrelevant. What matters is that the 'termination'—like the rest of his life—should be properly spent.

There are many ways of telling lies including the erection of picturesque but useless apparatus. The patient may want to see me because he feels that I have never told him lies; in this desperate situation he is anxious to hear the truth and to tell it—including the hate or love he *really* feels.

I have read a psycho-analytic paper in which the writer said that in cases where death was certain the analyst should give up making interpretations and resort to reassuring and comforting statements. I would not want to be told nice stories, whether they were psycho-analytical or religious or any other variety of pleasurable and gratifying seductions. I think that if I had never known the truth or wanted to hear the truth before, I would want to hear it in a serious situation. It is questionable whether any patient ever comes to a psycho-analyst unless they feel the situation is desperate; it is usually a last resort when everything else has failed. So in spite of appearances to the contrary the whole weight of the experience when a patient comes to see an analyst suggests that the patient himself feels that he needs a powerful injection of truth even though he may not like it.

What is your assessment of the job of psycho-analyst? I have already suggested that it would not be much use being invited to tell various forms of agreeable lies; not would I want to terrify anyone by telling him frightening stories about his possibly having a fatal disease. Although it may seem theoretical, or even philosophical, I find it easier to fall back on the feeling that I am called upon to make the person familiar with a particular aspect of truth. I know that is an unsatisfactory statement; Bacon summed it up in a famous essay: "'What is truth' said jesting Pilate, and would not wait for an answer". But I think that most people know what I mean when I say it is safest to feel that one is falling back on as near as one can get to the truth. At least one becomes part of a distinguished company of scientists, painters, musicians and other artists; they are all attempting to display some aspect of the truth. I say 'all'; I mean all those who belong to the distinguished company. Imitation musicians, imitation painters and scientists there are in plenty. There is something unsatisfactory about the imitation, and if it is unsatisfactory to oneself it doesn't require a great deal of imagination to suppose that it would be unsatisfactory to a patient who is in a desperate situation.

The truth. What does it look like? Who wants to be confronted with a 'trompe l'oeil' representation of Paradise? Such confections are pardonable to an agent selling us our earthly home, but not for our eternal home — our Self. In every job the first stage is an imaginative conjecture. The engineer building a dam has to have an imaginative conjecture about where the dam would do the most good, or where it might do the most harm if it were badly built. Later, the imaginative conjecture might become a rational conjecture; the secondary plan might be more workable than the first. In analysis one's first guess as to what the patient wants could be replaced by something which could be drafted on a piece of paper. Ask yourself what these various stages are before you would be prepared to turn these conjectures into a picture in your own mind of what you think the effect would be if you said something to that particular patient.

I think that a revised Grid — not to take the place of the first one — would be useful for a practising analyst to be able to consider how 'a pattern emerges'.* I find it useful to consider that the stages are an imaginative conjecture, a rational conjecture, a pictorial image — the sort of thing you can see in dreams and even 'paint' in a verbal version of a pictorial image. That also might come into your grid as part of the progress from O — when you know nothing whatever about the patient — and one tenth or one hundredth of a second later when you begin to have an idea of who or what has entered your consulting room. A minute later the shadowy impression might become more solid, 'three-dimensional'. You can invent this grid for yourself — the one which seems to come closest to your actual experience in analysis. It could also be applied to a scientific paper or to a lecture. The criterion, whether it is true, should also apply, but this time to something which is more aesthetic, as if you were engaged on a work of art. A scientific paper should remind you of real people; it should not be so boring, so unaesthetic that it becomes a pain in your mind to read it. We have a difficult job; even the impromptus in the analysis, the interpretations that we give, would be all the better if they stood up to aesthetic criticism. I hope that does not sound too much like Satan rebuking sin — I am well aware that my own interpretations, spoken or written, cannot pass these tests. But there is no reason why yours should not. You do not have to be limited by the limitations of your lecturers, teachers, analysts, parents. If you are, there is no room for growth.

*see p. 79